Starting & Running a Sandwich-Coffee Bar

Visit our How To website at www.howto.co.uk

At **www.howto.co.uk** you can engage in conversation with our authors - all of whom have 'been there and done that' in their specialist fields. You can get access to special offers and additional content but most importantly you will be able to engage with, and become a part of, a wide and growing community of people just like yourself.

At **www.howto.co.uk** you'll be able to talk and share tips with people who have similar interests and are facing similar challenges in their lives. People who, just like you, have the desire to change their lives for the better - be it through moving to a new country, starting a new business, growing their own vegetables, or writing a novel.

At **www.howto.co.uk** you'll find the support and encouragement you need to help make your aspirations a reality.

How To Books strives to present authentic, inspiring, practical information in their books. Now, when you buy a title from How To Books, you get even more than just words on a page.

Stephen Miller

Starting & Running a

An **Insider Guide** to setting up
your own successful business...

Sandwich-coffee Bar

Published by How To Books Ltd,
Spring Hill House, Spring Hill Road,
Begbroke, Oxford
OX5 1RX United Kingdom.
Tel: (01865) 375794. Fax: (01865) 379162
info@howtobooks.co.uk
www.howtobooks.co.uk

First published 2002
Reprinted 2004, 2005, 2006, 2007 and 2008
Reprinted with amendments 2009
Second edition 2011

British Library Cataloguing in Publication Data.
A catalogue record for this book is available from the British Library.

ISBN 978 1 84528 465 7

Cover design by Baseline Arts Ltd, Oxford

Produced for How To Books by Deer Park Productions, Tavistock
Typeset and design by Baseline Arts Ltd, Oxford
Printed and bound in Great Britain by Bell & Bain Ltd, Glasgow

NOTE: The material contained in this book is set out in good faith for
general guidance and no liability can be accepted for loss or expense
incurred as a result of relying in particular circumstances on statements
made in this book. Laws and regulations are complex and liable to
change, and readers should check the current position with the relevant
authorities before making personal arrangements.

Contents

Acknowledgments

Firstly I would like to thank How To Books for giving me the opportunity to publish this book, and in particular Nikki Read for many helpful comments, particularly in the early, embryonic stages.

In addition I have received considerable assistance, generally freely and obligingly given, from a wide range of local and national government bodies on a whole range of subjects such as employment law, VAT, National Insurance, planning, environmental health, food hygiene, business start ups and so on. I would say to any budding sandwich-coffee bar proprietor that they should have no qualms whatever about contacting their local authority or any government body for help with any such matters. Just be prepared to persist until you get through to the right person.

I would also like to mention some individuals all of whom provided advice and assistance on a wide range of topics: Simon Ambrose, Bill Dixon, George Gretton, Iain Hunter, Sandy MacCalman, Martin McMenigall, Ross McNaughton, David Miller, Edward Miller and Ottilie Miller. Molli Burrell deserves a special mention for having greatly encouraged the idea during an enjoyable writing course on Lanzarote. Finally my heartfelt gratitude to Judy without whom…

Preface

It has become a cliché that job security for life is now a thing of the past. A variety of people, at various ages and stages of their working lives, find themselves without a job – or in a job which is stressful because of the extra demands placed on them by companies concerned about profit margins in an increasingly competitive world.

Many people cast around for ways of escape to new work situations which can offer them security, control and a reasonable income – and if possible some form of pension or asset for the future. This is the situation I found myself in twenty years ago. After considering all sorts of money-making ideas, from growing kiwi fruit to buying and letting out flats, my wife and I hit upon the idea of opening a sandwich-coffee bar.

It has proved to be a reliable and secure source of income. Not only that, but despite the challenges and the hard work, we have found it very satisfying to set up and run our own business. It is also stimulating to try out new ideas and fine-tune the operation in response to the ever-changing demands of increasingly knowledgeable customers and new developments in the food and catering industries.

Oh – and by the way, do you have children? If so, you will find that working on a Saturday or during school holidays will give them a protected but authentic introduction to the real world of work.

Throughout this book I will refer to 'sandwich-coffee bars' by which I mean a sandwich bar with or without a seating area which also sells coffee. However, this expression doesn't really tell the whole story. 'Sandwich-coffee bar' should also be taken as potentially including:

- ◆ **Café/coffee bar.** Many sandwich-coffee bars have substantial café-style seating areas allowing people to relax in comfort over a cappuccino or an Earl Grey tea. These facilities can range from a bar along one wall plus one table and a few stools to a substantial area with ten or more tables.
- ◆ **Delicatessen ('sandwich deli').** You will find that many people who started with a delicatessen diversify by introducing sandwiches and coffee and creating a sitting area. The obvious advantage is that they already have much of the infrastructure in place for selling sandwiches.

You will also find places which sell sandwiches and coffee but specialise in tortilla wraps or a range of home-made soups. I have come across a number of newsagents' shops and bookshops which have successfully created mini sandwich-coffee bars in underused corners of their premises. This makes double sense because it's an additional facility for existing customers and it attracts more people who might buy newspapers or magazines. And don't forget the internet café scene. Really the possibilities and permutations are endless. *However, what is beyond doubt is that there is an insatiable demand for bread with interesting food inside and good quality coffee.*

> **For day-time take-away food the sandwich is king. Have a range of other products by all means, but I guarantee none will do as well as the ever popular sandwich. And trying to sell coffee without sandwiches and cakes is almost always shown to be commercially unviable.**

As a realistic business proposition a sandwich-coffee bar has a number of advantages over much of the competition.

1. People have to eat so there's always a certain assured level of demand

This certainly can't be said of every kind of business, many of which suffer from uncertain and changing demand. Dot com. Need I say more?

2. The level of demand for take-away food in the 'affordable luxury' category has increased dramatically in recent years

The cake has increased in size. There is a lot of competition but there's always room for new outlets so long as the quality of the product and the service is high. In truth quite a few places still suffer from the British affliction of low standards of quality and service in the catering field. So the scope for success is considerable – it's really up to you.

3. Good quality sandwich-coffee bars are virtually recession-proof

This is not true of restaurants, many of which suffer badly when there is an economic downturn. Indeed, at such times sandwich-coffee bars benefit by picking up custom from people no longer able to justify the expense of a restaurant meal as often as in the past.

4. You don't need any formal qualifications

Having said that, unless you have recently trained in catering, you will have to attend a course in food hygiene. In addition if you have never been self-employed before you will have to learn some new skills – book-keeping, VAT returns, tax and employment rules and regulations. But don't worry: you really don't need to be a brain surgeon to get the hang of what you need to know. A lot of it is common sense and people in the relevant official departments are keen to help. In addition a lot of the work can be done online.

5. You can have a life outside working hours

True, you will have to be up fairly early in the morning, but most sandwich-coffee bars close any time between 3 and 5 pm. A lot of your customers may well work in offices so it might not be necessary to open at weekends. Some do, some don't. In the case of a husband and wife team it is perfectly feasible for one of you to have another job and help out in the shop at times that suit you – possibly opening up in the morning or doing some of the book-keeping in the evening.

This book is mainly about small independent outlets. However, once you've set up your first shop there's nothing to stop you taking on the world. Quite a few places have done this very successfully – 'Pret A Manger' and 'O'Brien's' to mention but many hundreds of units. If that is your aim this book will still be relevant because if you don't know the ins and outs of running one shop you're going to have a very hard time indeed building an empire.

Your own niche market

I'd like to tell you about an experience I had soon after my wife and I opened our first place which taught me an important lesson. I was working with my wife in the middle of the afternoon. An older man in dirty overalls eased himself into the shop. His suspicious expressions and uneasy body language made it clear he was doubting the wisdom of entering our establishment.

Me: 'Can I help you?'
Him: 'Eh, you gotta cheese sandwich?'
Me: 'Certainly. What kind of cheese would you like?. We've got Brie, Cambozola, Jarlsberg, Bavarian smoked, Edam, Gouda or undyed Cheddar.'
Him (after listening to the list with increasing and barely contained frustration) : 'Aw I dunno son, I just want a cheese sandwich.'

I wasn't sure how to respond to this. I felt, to use that ugly word, deskilled. There was an awkward silence. He then asked if we had any soup. When I told him, tentatively by now, that the soup that day was home-made broccoli and stilton he looked at me in horror and with a parting 'Nah, nah' walked out of the shop shaking his head, never to return.

To rub salt in the wound he went across the road to a long-established sandwich bar which my wife and I had rather sniffily dismissed as any kind of serious competition. It was actually closed with the front shutter half down. But the man was too hungry and fired up to be put off. I watched in horror as he ducked under the shutter and gesticulated urgently to the owner who was clearing up inside.

Through our front window I could see them having a lengthy chat punctuated by many violent hand gestures by our erstwhile customer. It was clear beyond doubt that he had made the short but irrevocable journey from potential customer to leading critic. A few minutes later he walked off pumped up full of righteous indignation. He was clutching a small brown paper bag which doubtless contained a basic cheese sandwich (garishly dyed orange cheddar with thickly spread cheap margarine, I thought with disdain) which he would find entirely sufficient for his needs.

This exchange left me feeling helpless and mystified. Surely I had done everything in my power to provide a good service for a potential new customer? What else could I have done? I racked my brains but I had to face the fact that my best wasn't good enough. Myriad thoughts of financial failure, personal inadequacy and an early exit from the sandwich making business crowded my mind.

All nonsense of course. Put all thoughts of class divisions, elitism and political correctness right out of your mind. The simple lesson of my little anecdote is that in coming to the market you must have your own particular identity – and realise that it will not appeal to everybody. You might want to target the man in the overalls – fine – it's a big (though declining) market. You might aim for upmarket business types, trendy students or camera-toting tourists or a combination of them. None of these choices is right or wrong, good or bad. What is important is not to think that you can appeal to them all – you can't and frankly it would be a dull world if you could because every town and city centre would be full of identical sandwich-coffee bars. Have a plan, be prepared to take a few risks – and follow your instincts.

A growing industry

Sandwiches are big business. According to some press reports they constitute 'the fastest growing food sector.' In America it is apparently the case that 50% of food expenditure goes on eating out. In Britain it's under 30% – so, given our habit of following American trends there is clearly room for growth. And lots of people can have a slice of the action. If you have a feel for food, are prepared to be flexible, hard working and consistent then, whilst you probably won't become a millionaire, you have every chance of making a reasonable income, building up an asset of some value and getting to know a wide variety of people along the way. I hope that my experiences help you to avoid some of the inevitable pitfalls and make you aware of the endless possibilities for making a go of it.

Stephen Miller

CHAPTER ONE

Planning Your Business

1. The new marketplace – mainly good news

A bigger cake

There has been a significant cultural change in the recent past. Eating out during the day has become much more than just attending to a physical need. It has become a positive pleasure which increasing numbers of people indulge in – and not just at lunchtime. You will see people snacking or drinking coffee at all times of the day. And they are constantly on the lookout for new places with interesting ideas to tempt them. They also have much greater spending power – hence the demise of the packed lunch. This all means that the size of the cake has increased enormously.

The other side of the coin, however, is that there has been an explosion of new outlets of every kind, shape and size to cater for this demand. Quality levels have gone up in leaps and bounds as customers have become increasingly discerning. *Increased demand has led to more demanding customers.*

Never forget though – there's always room at the top.

More potential locations to choose from

Nowadays you'll come across neighbourhood sandwich-coffee bars in areas of town, away from the centre, where they would not have been commercially viable up until fairly recently. This is partly explained by the increased and widespread demand for quality food to take away.

However, economic changes have also played a part. When I moved to Edinburgh in the 1970s there were neighbourhoods packed with small greengrocers', haberdashers', butchers', fishmongers' and other specialist shops, often family businesses. In addition there was a trend for banks, building societies, solicitors and estate agents to open branches in outlying areas of cities. So small units in areas well away from city centres were much in demand.

Things are very different now. The advent of shopping centres and the rationalisation which has taken place in the financial and business sectors have led to the closure of many of these units. As a result many small and medium sized shops have been coming onto the market in recent times. Such areas are often particularly good for the small independent since they may not be capable of producing the level of turnover required by larger operations which by their nature are less flexible and adaptable.

These patterns have been repeated to a greater or lesser extent throughout Britain. Accordingly there is now greater scope for acquiring all sorts of properties at many price levels in a wide variety of locations. Despite this, the prime sites will always attract a lot of competition.

> **Setting up in business is never an easy option, but the demand is there – and there are properties available from which to trade. First though you have to ask yourself some pretty tough questions and carry out a fair bit of research. This is essential to discover if it's for you and you're for it – and if it's a viable proposition in your neck of the woods.**

2. Assessing your suitability

Are you physically fit?

Running a sandwich-coffee bar hands-on involves a great deal of physical activity requiring a lot of energy. You will be on your feet most of the day. For this reason good posture is very important if you are to avoid back pain. By the end of the week you may well have collected the odd cut or bruise.

Imagine the scene:

You arrive at the shop at 7.30 am. You're hoping that the rolls and bread have been delivered and that the lettuce, tomatoes and cucumbers have arrived. (If not there'll be urgent phone calls to the offending supplier.) You put the different breads in their baskets and start washing and slicing the vegetables. Sandwich ingredients stored in the fridge or the bottom of the serve-over unit have to be brought out and put attractively on display.

For the first part of the day you're getting ready for lunchtime:

◆ mixing mayonnaises (add a few fresh herbs to good quality mayonnaise to create some really special accompaniments for meats and other ingredients)

◆ preparing some of your own ingredients e.g. salsa and coleslaw (so simple and so much nicer than the processed stuff)

◆ preparing and packaging sandwiches for the shelf

◆ receiving supplies, putting them away in cupboards

◆ paying the window cleaner

◆ running to the bank for change

◆ serving some customers

◆ making sure the soup is heating up gradually, ready for lunchtime – don't forget to stir it or it will stick to the bottom of the soup kettle!

At lunchtime you will, you hope, be under serious pressure as the crowds arrive. The work is relentless and the noise of people talking all at once around you can be overwhelming. And what about your own lunch break? Well the staff have to have theirs so basically you just fit yours in if and when time allows. After the lunchtime rush you then have to concentrate on:

◆ the clearing up, the clearing up and the clearing up

◆ the telephone ordering (if you're lucky you can sit down to do this)

◆ serving a steady trickle of customers (and don't complain that they're keeping you off your work – they're the reason you're there!)

◆ remaining reasonably polite while yet another eager salesman comes in to explain to you why his cakes are better than the ones you're currently selling

◆ dealing with numerous points about the shop raised by an EHO (environmental health officer) during an unannounced (naturally) visit. This thankfully is exceptional.

◆ re-stocking the drinks shelves

◆ wiping the tables, cleaning the sides and spraying them with anti-bacterial fluid

◆ finally, sweeping and cleaning the floor and organising the rubbish so that you're ready to do it all over again tomorrow.

On your morning off you can go to the cash and carry to stock up on fizzy drinks, boxes of chocolate bars, crisps and so on. And what about the book-keeping – evenings or weekends perhaps?

Be honest, could you take it?

You need to be physically fit because you will spend a lot of time on your feet, working under pressure much of the time.

Do you like people?

In the course of a day you will come into contact with a great many people, some of whom you know and like, others you've never met before and a few who might be obnoxious. In all cases it is essential for you to smile and be pleasant and make time for some small talk.

Will you be able to cope diplomatically with someone who wants to give you chapter and verse about what they did at the weekend, when over their shoulder you can see a large queue of impatient people, short of time and food, building up?

It's true with most jobs, but especially when dealing directly with the public, that you must leave your troubles at the door when you come in. After all, you do want customers to come back. Sudden outbreaks of moodiness create a bad atmosphere and if repeated can undoubtedly be bad for business. This can be a major problem with a small minority of staff, an important point which I will deal with in Chapter Eight.

> **Being able to develop a quick and easy rapport with customers helps to make them feel welcome and comfortable – and more likely to come back in the future.**

Can you cope with all eventualities?

One day you will have somebody explaining to you how to clean the condenser in the dairy unit; the next, a pest control expert lecturing you on the private lives of mice and the one after that a salesman wearing the kind of back-of-the-throat-catching after-shave (now banned in some Californian restaurants), using his powers of persuasion to get you to switch your mayonnaise order to his company. At times you will pine for a job like theirs which simply requires you to be knowledgeable in one particular area.

The buck stops with you. If a member of staff phones in sick you will have to accept that your plan to do a bit of book-keeping is doomed and head for the shop right away.

> **It's your show. If somebody calls in sick or – worse still doesn't turn up, you'll have to sort it out – and if necessary step into the breach yourself.**

Are you happy to spend lots of time thinking about money?

Whether it's BP, Marks and Spencer or your small business, money is what it's really all about. You might love what you're doing but if it's not making a reasonable profit there really isn't any point in doing it. To be honest you'll know pretty quickly if the venture is going to be financially viable. Assuming it is you will still have to monitor the finances closely on a daily basis and learn how to *make money and not waste it*. Take one small example:

Are you going to have your windows professionally cleaned on a regular basis? Or are you or one of your staff going to do it? Before you answer, bear in mind that a window cleaning bill of say, £5 a week, over the course of a year amounts to £260. That's a lot of sandwiches and cups of coffee. And don't forget that everybody else from the butcher to the taxman gets their money come what may, so any new spending decisions affect the bit at the end that comes to you.

On the other hand you would have to invest in some materials; and of course it may not present a very good image to the outside world to see the boss up a ladder with a squeegee (though some people might admire the dedication). You might also find that some employees would baulk at doing this.

It may seem a minor point but, as you can see, every decision has to be thought through and money will invariably be the top priority.

> For what it's worth I think you *should* have your windows professionally cleaned. It's tax deductible, the window cleaner will do it better than you (in all weathers) and who knows, he might just become a customer....

Are you genuinely interested in food?

Are you enthusiastic about food or is eating just another bodily function?

◆ Do you know when an avocado is just right for use in a sandwich?
◆ It is possible to make good sandwiches with tinned tuna. But how would you rate tinned salmon?
◆ When you're asked if the prawns defrosted yesterday are still OK, will you be able to give a quick response with confidence at half past eight in the morning?
◆ Which kind of apple will the customer be more impressed by, Golden Delicious or Braeburn?

The fact is that a lot of the food you get in the better sandwich bars nowadays is on a par with reasonably good restaurant food – and to be able to compete you need to have a passion for food, as well as a good working knowledge of it.

It is possible for competent people to run some reasonably successful businesses even though the principal product holds no particular interest for them. I had an uncle who ran a successful operation selling fireplaces in much this way. But honestly, food is different. Whilst facts about the correct installation of marble fireplaces can be learned, dealing with food involves skills of creativity, taste and judgement which are more personal and instinctive. In the food business nowadays you have to be open to new flavours (guava, ostrich) and new combinations of old ones (sardines with tarragon).

> **You have to be interested in food because many of your customers will be.**

You only have to look at the industry which has built up around TV cookery programmes to know how much the public's interest has grown. The market is undoubtedly there and is increasing, but it's a demanding one. You will need to provide a service that is just that bit different to attract people's attention and persuade some of them to become regular customers. Without a feel for food and its possibilities this will be much more difficult. If you have any kind of catering qualification all to the good, but it is not essential.

Can you handle wasting perfectly good food?

Running a business challenges everyone in different ways. In my own case I thought it might be getting up early in the morning or possibly having to deal with staff problems. True, there have been times when these things have been challenging. *However, the thing I find hardest to accept is throwing out perfectly good food.*

There are, of course, strategies both for avoiding waste and for dealing with it when it does occur (see Chapter Five) – but sometimes there's no way round it. When this happens you just have to accept it and see it as one more aspect of running a business. You must at all costs avoid the temptation to find ways of disguising ageing food and offloading it onto an unsuspecting public. They're no more stupid than you are.

> **Selling perishable goods is not an exact science – you have**
> **to be able to live with some degree of waste.**

3. Doing your research

There is a lot of work to do before you sell your first sandwich. Up to this point in your life you have no doubt patronised numerous sandwich bars, cafés and similar outlets. But then it was different. Your interest was that of a customer not the potential proud proprietor of such an establishment. You must now put lots of sandwich bars and the things they sell under the microscope in order to help you formulate your own plan. You should:

1. Test drive lots of sandwich-coffee bars

Buy sandwiches, toasted sandwiches, tortilla wraps, microwave snacks, cakes and so on from a variety of outlets. Take them home, take them apart, see what's in them, think about portion size, eat them, assess the flavour quality, check the packaging and labelling for practicality and user friendliness and generally assess them to see in what ways and to what extent they would fit in with your embryonic scheme of things.

Make notes. You should quickly build up a list of things to avoid. Also try to collect as many menus as possible and go through them with a fine toothcomb for ideas.

Contact *International Sandwich and Snack News* (formerly known as *Sandwich and Snack News*), a very informative trade magazine which encourages you to 'Stay in touch with your market through your industry magazine.' Ask them to send you out a free sample copy and pick up ideas from them. If you're convinced it's for you, become a subscriber. The annual fee is currently £55 and the magazine is published six times a year. The magazine upholds the aims and objectives of the British Sandwich Association which essentially amount to promoting good standards, better knowledge and bigger sales of sandwiches. Subscribers have access to a Free Advice Line run by the British Sandwich Association. They also receive other magazines about coffee and cafe culture as well as the European scene. The contact address for The British Sandwich Association is Association House, 18c Moor Street, Chepstow NP16 5DB. Tel 01291 636333. www.sandwich.org.uk

2. Be aware of prices

One of the most important features of running a successful operation is getting the pricing right. It is also one of the most difficult, especially when you're starting up and might not feel confident about accurately valuing what you provide. It's impossible to recommend specific amounts to be charged for particular types of sandwich; there are far too many regional variations and, of course, prices never stay still.

It's a balance between what the customer is prepared to pay and what will deliver you a reasonable profit margin. You might come up with the best sandwich of all time but if you have to sell it for £10.00 to make a profit people won't buy it.

This is an ongoing task since naturally the cost of supplies goes up from time to time and you will probably have to impose a rise in the price of your core products once a year at least.

Don't forget also the ancillary things like bars of chocolate and cans of juice – you really don't want to find out that a can of Coke is 5p cheaper in your place than everybody else's. Or 5p more expensive. People will be prepared to pay more for the things which are uniquely yours like sandwiches if they feel the quality justifies it, but they will feel hard done by if the privilege of eating your wonderful sandwiches also means they have to pay more for cans of juice than they used to pay in the place next door.

Thanks to the internet it is possible to visit a variety of price comparison sites to obtain a picture of what people are paying to suppliers and what different sandwich-coffee bars – many of which have websites – are charging their customers.

This kind of information can be useful as a general guide when you're starting out. It can also be helpful when you are working out figures for your business plan. However, as you become established it's more relevant to be aware of the prices being charged by places in your immediate vicinity. As you become known in the area this can become awkward – you don't want to go into your competitor's place and ask them what they charge for a chocolate bar! Don't be afraid to ask friends or new employees to spy on your behalf. Do remember though to compare like with like. A grocer's shop will probably charge less for a can of juice than you; the kiosk at the cinema a great deal more.

3. Visit as many sandwich-coffee bars as possible

Sit in and take ages over a cappuccino and cake. Go back for seconds. Watch the staff (discreetly of course). Are they smartly dressed and groomed? If they have some kind of corporate image are you impressed by it or do you think those baseball caps look just a touch tacky? Do they seem more interested in talking to each other about what they did last night than being alert and responsive to customers' needs?

Watch the boss. Is he or she enjoying their work or does he look furtive, harassed and exhausted? Does it all seem like a happy ship? Why? Why not? Is the place clean? When the staff prepare food are you reassured that they are observing good hygiene standards? Does there appear to be a sensible layout to the shop?

What about the customers – do they look content or are they a bit disgruntled? If it's lunchtime it may well be busy but is there a reasonably efficient system for dealing with the demand? In general, what is the atmosphere in the shop like? Do you feel comfortable? Do you like the music? Is it too loud? What about the decor? Are there any strong aromas – pleasant and/or unpleasant?

These and many more questions must be asked to provide you with the kind of information you need in coming to decisions about starting up your own operation. As you carry out your detective work you should be asking yourself two main questions:
- ◆ **Would I like to be responsible for running an operation like this?**
- ◆ **What changes would I make in order to provide a better service and create my own distinctive style?**

As you deal with these questions a picture should be growing in your mind of the kind of operation you would like to have.

Draw diagrams of imaginary shops, make lists of the types of equipment you will need, think of colour schemes, seating arrangements and so on. Although you will be concentrating on the major issues such as the quality of the food and drink, it is also a good idea even at this stage to be thinking about some finishing touches which would make your place that little bit different – always try to stand out from the crowd. It might be some pictures, or an exterior sign. Don't just copy other sandwich-coffee bars and cafés but rather do a bit of lateral thinking with your own fertile imagination.

Visits other towns and cities to see what other people are doing. Even if you pick up one solid idea from such an outing then the trip will have been well worth it. Go to London. Many new trends start there. Just walk about and try to experience as many places as possible. Be ruthless. Look at a place from the outside and if it's clear it's not your sort of operation give it a miss and go on to one of the many that will be more relevant to you. If you don't do this you'll just get bogged down.

Although you may well wish to start up a small independent operation, do go and have a look at the big chains as well. They didn't get where they are now without a lot of good, well thought out and practical ideas.

Finally, make use of the internet. Put words such as 'sandwich', 'coffee', 'soup', 'take-away' or 'café' into a search engine and see what wild and wacky things you come up with from around the world.

4. The legal structure of the business

Sole trader

If you're unattached, becoming a sole trader is the obvious answer when you're setting up a new small business. It's straightforward from a legal, tax and accounting point of view. It also means you're answerable to no-one. What you earn is yours – after everyone from HMRC to the window cleaner has been paid, of course. Policy and strategy meetings are a breeze!

If you trade under a name other than your own you are required to display your name and address at your premises and on stationery.

> **Being a sole trader is the sensible non-bureaucratic choice for many single people in business for the first time.**

Partnership

If you are married or in a relationship then you could still operate as a sole trader if your other half isn't going to be involved in the new venture. However, forming a legal business partnership to underpin your new business is an attractive option from a variety of angles and is something which many couples do. The degree of involvement of a partner can be very small. It could be the odd bit of book-keeping or an occasional trip to the cash and carry. Equally it could be full 50% participation in all aspects of the business. Your accountant will prepare accounts which split profits in the most financially advantageous way.

◆ It is no bar to being a partner that somebody is in full- or part-time employment elsewhere.

◆ It is normal and desirable to have a written partnership agreement which your solicitor can prepare. Though not a legal requirement your bank may well insist on it.

◆ There can of course be tax advantages to a couple entering into partnership. For instance, when the income of the business is attributable to an individual it might attract tax at the top rate whereas it may well not if split between two partners.

◆ On a more general note it seems appropriate that two people involved in a venture should each have a financial stake in it. Hopefully it will become a progressively more valuable asset as the years go by.

◆ In the event of divorce each partner's share of the business will be simpler to assess.

◆ By setting up a partnership you are creating a legal entity which your children can join in the future if you and they wish.

It sounds rosy but don't forget that partners take on all the responsibilities of the business and have to bear losses as well as share in profits. There is also 'joint and several liability' for the financial obligations of the business. This means that a creditor is entitled to seek recovery of the whole of a debt from one partner. Put another way, if you are in a three-person partnership and your partners disappear you will be legally responsible for all the debts of the business partnership. You will have the right to recover any money paid out beyond your share but this might not be worth much.

This liability is one reason why, if you ever consider bringing one of your children or anybody else into the partnership, that person should be given detailed financial information about the business to enable them to make a fully informed choice. There are some circumstances where a new partner could be responsible for pre-existing debts. Prospective new partners should be told to obtain independent legal advice (yes, even your children) before being expected to make any kind of commitment.

The names of the current partners together with an address where documents can be served should be displayed on your headed paper or at your business premises.

Being in partnership has a variety of advantages for people who go into business together. It's particularly flexible for couples, but it can be quite onerous too.

Limited company

Experience and professional advice have led me to the view that it is not a good idea for someone starting out in business to do so by means of forming a limited company. For a start, it involves more bureaucracy than being a sole trader or being in partnership.

For instance, you have to prepare annual accounts and annual returns which must be lodged with your local Companies House. Failure to lodge accounts on time can constitute a breach of the criminal law. Do you really need this extra pressure at a time when you will have so much else on your mind?

There are certain benefits which do accrue to company directors – company cars for example – but these have come under close scrutiny by the Chancellor in recent years. It is true that there is limited liability in the event of business failure. However when setting up the finances for your new venture your bank will protect their loan to you by taking a legal charge (in Scotland a standard security) over the business premises or your house or by means of a personal guarantee. There's no escaping them!

Incorporation is best considered later on, if your operation expands considerably. This is the stage when the benefits such as more advantageous tax rates are greater.

Setting up a limited company is a specialised area for which good professional advice is essential.

One other point to bear in mind: it is apparently quite a simple legal matter to go from being a sole trader or a partnership to being a limited company – but more complicated the other way round.

> **Taking on the responsibilities of a limited company is something to consider later on, when your business is expanding and the experts tell you that incorporation would be advantageous.**

A further legal entity is the **limited liability partnership**. This may be of interest to the small businessperson as being a cross between a partnership and a company. The limited liability partnership is itself liable for the debts run up by the business as opposed the individual members. However, as with a limited company, formal registration and the lodging of annual accounts will be necessary, so for the new business sole trader or partnership is probably still best.

Franchising

In simple terms becoming a franchisee involves paying somebody else for the right to use their concept. The advantages are fairly obvious:

◆ You will enjoy the immediate commercial benefits of trading under a well known, tried and tested brand.

◆ You will receive (certainly in the case of the bigger internationally known brand names) professional advice and support from an experienced management team for setting up and running the operation.

However, there are a fair number of disadvantages:

◆ High start-up costs. Take the case of one currently prominent franchisor of sandwich bars as an example. The total capital requirement in 2008 of buying the equipment, fitting out a shop, architects' fees and so on was estimated to be about €246,500 (approximately £210,000) for a unit of 1,000 sq ft. Serious money. What's more, although the franchisor in question says that they might be able to help with financing, you the franchisee would have to come up with up to half the initial outlay from your own resources. You might, of course, get a more favourable deal from another bank but it's a lot of money to lose if things don't work out.

Bear in mind also that these figures are based on leasehold premises. They do allow for legal fees and a quarter's rent but do not include the cost of any premium you might have to pay to acquire the lease. Needless to say, if you want to buy premises this will add dramatically to the costs involved.

◆ You will need to engage solicitors experienced in this specialised field to advise you on the franchise agreement which will govern your relationship with the franchisor.
◆ Lack of independence. Basically you have to do things their way. You might be able to introduce the odd bit of fine tuning here and there but you can forget any creative ideas of your own.
◆ When you come to sell, the franchisor will have the right to vet any potential new franchisees – in the same way as they will have vetted you. In this particular case they also have the right to match the best offer you receive and buy the business themselves. Whilst such terms are not the end of the world they could complicate things and be highly offputting for a potential purchaser at a time when you might be very keen to do a quick deal.

If you are serious about franchising – and this is a route which quite a lot of people follow – you should have a discussion with the franchising governing body, The British Franchise Association (tel: 01235 820470) to get more information. Their web site is www.thebfa.org/. Also try to speak to some franchisees to find out how the experience has been for them. You will probably gain the most valuable insights by doing this. My impression is that they work just as hard as other small business people but sometimes resent the restrictions placed on them when their hard work has paid off and the business is doing well a few years down the line. There are regular exhibitions on the subject of franchising and obviously it would be a good idea to attend some of them in order to help you to decide if it's for you.

Admittedly I'm biased, but if you are confident that you have a reasonably good idea you could almost certainly put it into practice for less money than franchisors are talking about. What's more it would be all yours – if you wanted to make changes you would be free to do so without somebody else complaining about it.

5. Going into business with friends

Is it a good idea to go into business with a trusted friend? (Well it certainly isn't a good idea to go into business with one you don't trust!)

There are undoubtedly some advantages.

◆ You would each bring different areas of experience and expertise to the venture.
◆ If problems arise they might be resolved more easily with the input of two people who can look at an issue from different angles.
◆ You could cover for each other to allow the business to continue operating safely when one of you takes a well earned holiday. This is not to be underestimated since a lack of decent holidays is one of the commonest bugbears of small businesspeople.
◆ Two bank accounts are bigger than one. Accordingly you may well be able to go for better premises with more sophisticated equipment than you could have done on your own.

There are however, undoubted pitfalls as well.

◆ By it's very nature a small business is not very big. Unless you and your friend see eye to eye on virtually everything then areas of disagreement will emerge. Even quite minor issues can cause controversy. My wife and I agreed on lots of things without quibble but could we agree on the right colour for the exterior of our second shop? It took weeks of discussion and humming and hawing and was only resolved by one person agreeing to something they were not very keen on. I wonder who?

> Husbands and wives are used to a bit of arguing over things like this – but friends? Probably not. The relationship isn't usually about such things. As always, money can be the biggest source of potential conflict, particularly decisions on how much to spend on particular items.

◆ You might get on tremendously well with someone and maybe even with their husband or wife, but what about your own spouse or partner? If, say, problems arise necessitating longer working hours and he or she feels that you are taking too much of the strain, might this not generate a lot of tension for your relationship as well as your business partnership?

◆ If the business doesn't succeed, with the best will in the world, your friendship will come under great pressure. You will find yourself in the position of having to try to unravel legal, business and financial matters with someone who was previously associated with carefree socialising over a few drinks.

I have known at least two lengthy friendships which foundered in a short space of time after a hotel venture, which the people concerned set up, ran into difficulties. Forewarned is forearmed.

For what it's worth my own view is that a small business such as a sandwich-coffee bar, especially one just starting up, is not generally big enough to accommodate two sets of people and their myriad ideas. I think it is well suited to husbands and wives but I prefer to keep my friends as friends and not become involved with them financially or businesswise. However, this is only my view and there are no doubt examples of friends successfully going into business together… I just can't think of any!

Going into business: advice and education

There are government-supported initiatives to encourage, assist and support new business start-ups throughout Britain.

In **England** contact Business Link, tel: 0845 6009006.

In **Wales** contact Business Connect, tel: 08457 96 97 98.

In **Scotland** contact Small Business Gateway, tel: 0845 6096611.

In **Northern Ireland** contact Business Link, tel: 02890 239090.

Your local Chamber of Commerce will have business start-up advisors who will be able to deal with frequently asked questions on the subject.

Check with local colleges. Some will run courses under the general heading of Business and Finance or Business Administration. Some courses will last a year and will provide a valuable introduction to many of the most important aspects of the business world. Financial assistance for such courses may be available.

In addition, contact your local council. They will almost certainly have details of other small business initiatives which may be of relevance to your situation. However, it is most unlikely that you will receive any form of financial assistance. Rather it will be a case of advice on starting a business or help to locate suitable properties. This could be extremely valuable for the novice. But if you already have experience of running a small business you probably know more about it than they do!

Financial contribution to the venture

How much hard cash should you put into your business? In my opinion there is no specific formula which can be neatly applied to this question. Banks have rules about what percentage they will lend (see page 25 for more information about banks). However, they do have some discretion. If you have a good record and are capable of being reasonably assertive then there is some leeway. In fact I have heard that some managers prefer it if instead of asking, the customer simply tells the bank what he or she wants.

I have known people in business who take the view that maximum pressure should be exerted on the bank to provide as much of a loan as possible. They will tell you that all of the most mega-successful businesspeople in the world have got where they are today by doing this and setting up their businesses 'with someone else's money.' Maybe so, but I'm sure lots of them have made mega losses as well. Anyway does this description relate to you? I doubt it.

> **The hard fact is that unless you have a lot of pull with the bank you will have to come up with a fair bit of money. The bank will see this as an important aspect of your commitment to the new venture, particularly so in light of recent financial crises.**

It follows that before you are in a position to go after particular properties you and/or your partner will need to have built up some savings. One of the reasons it is important to make contact with your bank at an early stage is so that, amongst other things, you have a clear idea of how much money you will need to contribute.

Given that the bank will want something I think the best answer to the question posed at the start of this section is: as little as the bank will reasonably accept.

> **Don't forget also that you should have some savings over and above what is required for the new venture. You're going to need a holiday at some point and the shop probably won't be able to finance this in the first year.**

CHAPTER TWO

Dealing with Your Professional Advisors

Getting the right people

You might think that setting up a sandwich-coffee bar is a small venture in the great scheme of things. Maybe so. However, to turn the dream into reality any new business, large or small, needs the expertise and support of a team of people with a variety of skills. What's more, it's important to have most of them in place before you make an irrevocable commitment to a particular unit – their roles are too important for them to be engaged at a later date when there is insufficient time to make properly considered choices.

One of the hard facts of small business life is that quite a lot of professional and other advisers tend to prefer dealing with bigger clients and customers. They make more money out of them. It's as simple as that. It follows that you should do all in your power to ensure that those people to whom you entrust your valuable business specialise in working for operations of your size.

> **When it comes to consulting the experts it's a case of horses for courses.**

Here's a list of the key players:
- Solicitors
- Accountants
- Architects
- Surveyors
- Bank Managers
- Insurance Brokers
- Environmental Health Officers
- Refrigeration Advisor
- Shopfitters, decorators, plumbers and electricians.

Some of them will become important components in your ongoing business even if you only need to consult them occasionally. It is very much in your interests to have good working relationships with all of them.

Instructing a solicitor

Do you already have a solicitor? Is it the one who bought your house for you a few years ago? It could well be that he or she doesn't know a great deal about the ins and outs of setting up small businesses. This really matters because it is a specialist area. Make contact, explain your plans and ask quite openly if the solicitor has much experience of handling the affairs of small businesspeople. Of course solicitors will not be keen to turn away business so you might find yourself having to make a judgement about his or her suitability. *This won't be the last time you have to make important decisions about matters you don't necessarily know a lot about.*

Remember that personal recommendations from other people with small businesses can be invaluable. You could also contact the Law Society (see your local telephone directory for details or do a Google search) which keeps a register of solicitors with expertise in particular fields.

Once you have made a decision, have a meeting and discuss your ideas in detail. Your solicitor should be able to give you initial thoughts and advice in areas such as:
◆ purchasing or leasing properties
◆ acquiring going concerns
◆ the legal structure of the business
◆ finance
◆ employment law
◆ preparation or updating of wills to take account of your new asset
◆ (and, if you're lucky) insights into good and bad locations based on years of being involved with the commercial life of your particular area.

In addition, an experienced solicitor should be able to recommend other advisors in the areas of accountancy, architecture and insurance. If you're going to be running a business for the first time you may not have any contacts in these fields.

When you have a particular property in mind your solicitor will play a pivotal role in tying up the deal. You will probably be on the phone every day. The more he or she understands your vision the less explaining you will have to do when you are going through the critical phase of trying to secure a deal.

> **To be most effective your solicitor must have relevant experience and a full understanding of what exactly you are trying to achieve.**

Instructing an accountant

Put simply, your accountant's job is to ensure that you pay as little tax as legitimately possible. He or she is therefore a very important person in your universe. Whilst it's not absolutely essential it's highly desirable to instruct an accountant as early as possible. Your accountant can give you advice on a wide range of matters which may well need to be decided or acted upon prior to or very soon after you commence trading. These matters include:

◆ the most advantageous constitution of the business from a tax point of view
◆ the tax implications of you or your partner continuing to work as an employee
◆ registration for VAT
◆ keeping records; the aim here is to provide the accountant with as much information as possible in a form they find easy to process – this will save them time and you money
◆ suitable book-keeping systems
◆ PAYE and National Insurance
◆ tax rates, allowances, returns, dates of payment and self-assessment
◆ capital gains tax (when you come to sell the business).

As with your solicitor it is most important that your accountant should be used to dealing with small businesses and keen to do this kind of work. Apart from anything else, if you instruct someone who is used to dealing with larger companies you will receive larger bills. A personal recommendation is always a good idea but if this is not possible then you can contact the Institute of Chartered Accountants (see your local telephone directory for details or do a Google search).

Helping them to help you

One of the most common complaints accountants have about their clients is that they don't respond quickly when asked to provide financial information for the completion of accounts and tax returns, and when they do the information is often incomplete. This, of course, means that reminders have to be sent out and more work done. The irony of this is that the people who are trying to save money for their clients end up charging more because those self-same clients are too busy making sandwiches to bother with paperwork.

Your accountant's job is to ensure you don't pay too much tax. Your job is to give them the detailed information they need to achieve this – promptly.

**It really is in your interests to develop a good working relationship
with advisors such as your solicitor and accountant.**

Building good relationships

The hope is that your solicitor and accountant will get to know you and your business well over the years. This will be most important when there are new developments such as the acquisition of a second outlet. It will be equally true if you run into problems in your business life, such as a dispute with your landlord or a tax inspection. It is unlikely that you will go through a career in business without some such trauma. They will be on hand to give prompt and appropriate advice and assistance. *The more they know about your business history the better able they will be to achieve this in the shortest possible time.*

The legal and accountancy professions have become much more market-oriented and competitive in recent times. This has led to considerable differences in fees from firm to firm. As a result you do hear of people who regularly switch from one professional to another to save a few hundred pounds.

Whilst I well understand the objective of saving money I think it is more advantageous to the small businessperson to build up a good relationship over the years.

Talking about fees

Bear in mind also that most solicitors nowadays are perfectly happy to discuss their likely charges at the outset. Don't be afraid to ask. If a solicitor or accountant is not prepared to do this I doubt if they will be appropriate to look after the interests of a small business. Obviously they are not able to give an exact figure for a particular transaction because unpredictable things can happen. However, there should be no reason why you cannot be given a good idea of the likely costs – apart from anything else you will need these figures to help you put together your business plan.

**Develop a good relationship with solicitors and accountants
but don't be afraid to discuss matters such as fees and other charges.**

Using an architect

You will probably need an architect no matter how straightforward you think your particular venture is.

◆ You will have to establish for certain what the current lawful use of the premises is.
◆ You may require permission from your local planning authority to change the use of the premises. This can be a lengthy procedure – even when apparently simple and non-contentious.
◆ Unless you have no plans to alter the layout of the shop at all then you will need authority for any alterations you intend to carry out. These can be as seemingly minor as installing a small wash hand basin. Such alterations must comply with building regulations.

An architect can advise and assist with all of these matters. I must stress again the importance of establishing that your architect has experience of smaller commercial units – and don't forget to ask for an indication of cost at the outset.

Planning permission – change of use

One great advantage of sandwich-coffee bars with a limited amount of seating is that as a general rule they simply require retail use ('A1', or 'Class 1' in Scotland) which is effectively the same as a shop selling sweets. This is the most common use and is the easiest and least controversial one to obtain. There is a fair chance your chosen unit will already have it. What's more A1 use generally carries with it permission to sell, in addition to sandwiches, hot drinks, soup, toasted sandwiches and a limited amount of food cooked in one microwave cooker. These things are regarded as *ancillary* to the main use.

A word of warning: the attitude of the authorities can vary from place to place and some take a stricter line than others. If you sell nothing but cold sandwiches, chocolate bars and cans of soft drinks and have no seating whatsoever then undoubtedly you will only require A1 use. The use of the premises would obviously be retail. But, once you start adding on ancillary items such as soup and toasted sandwiches, especially if you have some seating, then there is an argument that the nature of the use of the premises is changing to something nearer a café/coffee shop or a bistro/restaurant. In this case you would require A3 use (Class 3 in Scotland). There are also restricted versions of A3 which allow for a limited amount of cooking on the premises.

Over the years I have spoken to various people in authority about when you need A3 and when A1 will suffice. When you try to pin them down they almost invariably start talking about a 'grey area'. The question really is what is the *essential and predominant* use of the premises. For many sandwich-coffee bars the answer is that it is a take-away selling cold food which also has some seating and a modest range of hot items such as coffee, soup and toasted sandwiches. In my experience the authorities will generally regard such use as falling within A1. They will probably insist that customers who ask should be allowed to use your toilet (assuming you do have some seating).

You should speak to your architect or contact the planning department at your local council offices and discuss your intentions with them. Do this sooner rather than later. What you must avoid at all costs is *assuming* A1 will be sufficient for your purposes and then being advised later, perhaps when you are up and running, that in fact you require A3. This could be a serious matter. If the planning department feel that the essential nature of the unit goes beyond a retail unit you will have to submit an application for A3 use. This may well involve the provision of customer toilets, observation of strict fire regulations, the installation of an effective ventilation system (if cooking food will be involved) and so on. The procedure is time-consuming and expensive and would certainly require the services of an architect.

Increasing the value of your asset

A3 use is appropriate for a wide range of catering outlets and potentially permits full-scale cooking on the premises. Such permission would almost certainly increase the value and desirability of your asset – whether or not you ever use the permission and whether you rent or buy. It would also mean you could expand the nature of the operation in the future without the hassle of an application for change of use.

This is not, however, a step to be taken lightly. Such applications involve the preparation of detailed architects' plans. Neighbouring residents or proprietors might lodge objections because of worries over the possible impact on their late night peace of a hot food take-away in the future. You could find yourself embroiled in a lengthy and costly process. In addition such permission usually only lasts for a set period of time such as five years before it needs to be used or renewed. It will be more complicated still if the property is in a conservation area or is part of a listed building.

If you want to go down this route it's essential to get your architect's advice on what will be involved as early as possible.

Using a surveyor

Everyone who acquires a business property will need the services of a surveyor. Their assessment of your chosen unit will be crucial in helping to determine some very important matters:

◆ the value of the property

◆ the appropriate level of rent/premium

◆ the amount you can borrow on the property, and consequently...

◆ the amount you will need to contribute from your own resources

◆ details of necessary repairs – which might limit resources available for equipment, etc.

Strange as it may seem though, remarkably few clients speak directly to this vital professional. Surveying is most often done through a solicitor or estate agent. This means that the expert report on the business and/or property which you are about to invest your money and dreams in is carried out by someone you don't know and probably won't even speak to. The report doesn't come direct to you but via the solicitor who may or may not ask all the questions you would like answered. Having said all this the surveyor is not the most important person in the equation and the present system does seem to work reasonably well, so I don't want to raise unnecessary concerns. It's just something you should bear in mind.

If you have made the right choice of solicitor then they should be able to make sure that a surveyor suitable to your requirements is instructed – and that the report deals with any particular matters of concern to you.

Personally, I have got to know one particular firm of surveyors quite well over the years. When I am interested in a property I instruct them myself, discuss the findings directly and then arrange for a copy to be sent to my solicitor. I can only say that this approach strikes me as more reassuring. It has an added benefit: if I simply have a property in mind but don't want to spend money on a survey I can phone them up for their thoughts on the place. If they have inspected the property in the past they are usually quite happy to give an indication of their findings. This all saves time and money and might be especially helpful later if you are interested in expanding your empire and want to check out potential second outlets.

A surveyor plays a vital role. Consider carefully the benefits of building a personal relationship rather than leaving it to solicitors or estate agents to deal with them.

Approaching a bank

When it comes to property the mantra may be 'Location, location, location' but for businesses in general it should be 'Money, money, money'. Enter your friendly but slightly paternalistic neighbourhood bank manager, peering sternly but benevolently at you with experienced eyes over his pince-nez. Well that's how it used to be. Nowadays you are more likely to be critically assessed by a number-crunching official. He or she might have a charming, smiling manner but it's probably been learnt at a series of seminars run by progressive-aggressive consultants appointed by the bank to make it more up to date and 'relevant'.

Regardless of how they do business, banks are crucial to any new business venture.

If you already have a bank with whom you have satisfactorily maintained an account for a few years then this should be your first port of call. You will be introduced to someone in the business section who will have the designation – 'Banking Relationship Manager' or something of the sort. If you don't have a relationship with a bank then your request for a loan will be treated with greater caution. They will almost certainly want to carry out credit checks. All of my remarks have to be read against the background of the recent turbulence in the world of banking which can only make obtaining loans more difficult and more expensive. That said, things are at last starting to get a bit easier and banks are under pressure to make loan facilities more readily available.

Your financial contribution

If you do not have any available money to invest in your business you will not persuade a bank to invest in it either. It is impossible to state categorically how much the bank will expect you to put in because banks' policies differ and, depending on your previous relationship, a bank might be persuaded to agree to a smaller than usual deposit.

If you buy your property, as a general indication, a bank will probably be prepared to contribute 70% of valuation, leaving you to find the remaining 30% plus the difference between the valuation figure and the price you actually pay to get the place if greater than valuation. The bank will expect you to provide the deposit from your own resources, not another loan.

So far as the fitting out costs are concerned, as a general guide, banks will probably look to you to contribute 50% from your own resources. The bank will probably want some security for their loan which will be greater than the actual amount borrowed. If, for instance, the cost of fitting out comes to £40,000 it is likely the bank will want security to the extent of around £55,000. This is because in the event of business failure and the security having to be realised (banks always look at the worst case scenario) the amount raised may be less than anticipated. The security is most likely to be your house or some other property but could also take the form of stocks and shares.

If you lease premises and you require funding simply to fit the shop out and/or pay for goodwill and fixtures and fittings the figures are likely to be similar – i.e. the bank will lend 50% of the costs on the basis of security cover along the lines mentioned above.

Dealing with the bank

Over the years I have heard many complaints about banks from friends and colleagues. If it's a question of persistent mistakes such as paying money into the wrong account or failing to cancel direct debits then I sympathise. Everyone makes the odd mistake but there is no excuse for repeated sloppiness and it should not be tolerated. However, on the general question of agreeing loans, extending overdrafts and so on I have to say that in 25 years I have had few difficulties.

Don't forget: banks are commercial operations. They are keen to do business but they are not going to make available loans if there is no realistic prospect of repayments being maintained. This would not be in anybody's interests – least of all someone dipping their toe into the commercial ocean for the first time.

Equally, if accounts do fall into arrears, whilst they should be sympathetic and constructive in their response, at the end of the day they will take action to recover money due to them.

If you follow certain simple rules in your dealings with banks they should be supportive of your venture in good times and bad – and such support really can be crucial.

1. Talk to the bank sooner rather than later

When starting out don't wait until you've got a particular property in mind and are under pressure to conclude a deal. It's important to get an idea of how much you can borrow, what the likely repayments will be and what the banks requirements are – business plan, type of survey and so on. This is equally true when, later on, you want to expand the business or acquire some new equipment. Make an appointment and let your bank know about your plans.

2. Use good psychology

Make the person you are dealing with feel important. Share your ideas and make it clear above all that you are looking to them for help and that you respect their opinions. Don't give the impression that you take them for granted. In a way it's all a bit false but it's also part of the game called Being In Business.

3. Let the bank know right away if there are problems

Once you're up and running it would be surprising if you didn't experience a bit of turbulence now and then. If you become aware that financial problems are in the offing make an appointment and explain the position. This will be greatly appreciated and it may well be that your bank will have the necessary experience to be able to make sensible suggestions as to what you can do to deal with the situation. Apart from anything else you need to know to what extent the bank will be prepared to help you out. Even if the problems are serious or indeed terminal, nothing will be gained by burying your head in the sand – least of all the support and co-operation of your banking advisor.

4. Deal promptly with requests for information

Each year your bank will ask to see your most recent set of trading accounts. In addition it will be in touch with you about the renewal of overdraft or other borrowing facilities. If you ignore such requests because you're 'too busy making a living' you will cause extra work and irritation and will make yourself appear unprofessional.

If you follow these simple rules then you are unlikely to encounter serious problems with your bank.

Not only that but you will probably find that obtaining a house mortgage or personal loan will be a bit easier – potentially very helpful since self-employed small business people sometimes find it harder to obtain such loans.

In my experience the people who run into difficulties with banks and complain about them the loudest have failed to follow these rules. I suspect some have an inbuilt prejudice against banks for some indefinable reason. If you have such feelings I suggest you get over them. You need banks. Of course, they need you too, so you shouldn't let them walk all over you.

Your business plan

In considering your application for a loan your bank will want to see a business plan. I'm sure many people not used to writing essays or reports will dread this particular requirement but really it's not something which should alarm you. There are many books which give advice on how to prepare a plan and these may well be helpful. Bear in mind that brilliant works of literature are not required and your plan can be quite simple and does not need to follow any particular style though there would be no harm in asking your bank if they happen to have any preferred layout.

The plan should not run to more than four or five pages. It should be neat, typed not handwritten, and easy to follow. The first page should be an 'elevator statement' – wonderful expression. It means a statement that is short enough to read in the time it takes to travel up to someone's office by elevator. You will also see it referred to as an 'executive statement'. Apart from your personal details it should contain the key elements, in bullet point format, of your business plan.

There are a number of important general points to bear in mind when writing a business plan.

1. The plan is at best a well-informed guesstimate

The banks are aware of this. But, they want evidence that you have realistically appraised the financial nuts and bolts of your new venture and that you can make out a solid case for a business which is going to be able to produce a reasonable turnover. If your figures produce an annual profit of £1000 or £1,000,000 then clearly you will have to go back to the drawing board. The estimated turnover and profit margin has to be realistic.

> **The banks don't know all the answers but they can tell the difference between a realistic proposition and pie in the sky.**

2. The expenditure side of the plan is the easy bit to estimate

We have all had to make bank loan repayments and pay electricity and telephone bills. When starting work on your business plan just try to make a list of every single thing you will have to spend money on; per week, per month or per year, whichever is easiest. Then convert all figures to annual. It's not straightforward, of course, because you don't necessarily know how many refrigerated units you will have nor how much electricity they will use (more than you think, I can tell you!).

Phone your local business electricity office and try to get an idea of likely annual charges from them.

Contact a supplier of meats or sandwich fillings or whatever and ask them about the price of their goods. See if they can give you an idea of what a small or medium sized sandwich bar spends on average.

Contact your local rating office, who should be able to tell you exactly what are the current charges applicable to your property – and don't forget to ask if there are any increases in the pipeline.

It won't be exact but it is possible to build up a reasonably accurate picture.

3. The income side is the hard part

Income really is a guesstimate. By this stage you will have carried out some initial research. Go back to a sandwich-coffee bar similar to the kind of operation you have in mind. Sit in your car for an hour or so at a busy time and a quieter time and count the number of people going in and out. Imagine the sort of selection of things they will buy and the average spend per customer, bearing in mind the prices you intend to charge. This will inevitably vary considerably from place to place. A chicken sandwich in central London will cost more than one in Halifax. It's impossible to generalise. Try to work out a daily take. Remember that for most operations catering to any significant extent for the office trade, takings on Saturdays and Sundays will be 30 or 40% lower than on weekdays.

Assuming you are going to make your own sandwiches (which most places do), work on a gross profit margin (i.e. retail cost to the customer less the cost of bread, filling and packaging) in the region of 60 to 70%. (If you decide to buy pre-prepared sandwiches in from a manufacturer you will probably receive a discount on retail price to the customer of between 30 and 40%).

You want a positive response from your bank so there is no harm in massaging the figures a little bit. *Anyway, since it's a guesstimate you might be right. Be sensible but be positive.*

4. Write about your vision for the venture

Demonstrate to the bank that you have thought through the why, the what, the where and the how. Draw a diagram of the shop showing the internal layout. Draw a map of the area surrounding the shop indicating the likely sources of business, offices, colleges, shopkeepers, passers-by and so on. Give details of the competition. Explain what you have that is just that bit different and which will attract customers away from some of the better-established places. Consider including some photographs. Give details of any relevant experience you and/or your partner have. Remember that many areas of work are relevant to running a business such as a sandwich-coffee bar: personnel work, book-keeping, accountancy and of course any involvement in catering or the hospitality industry generally. If you are a good amateur cook, interested in food, this too is relevant. Put it all together in a file or folder in a professional-looking style.

If you present your business plan to your bank in a clear easy-to-grasp way they are far more likely to be persuaded that you are the kind of well organised professional person to whom they should be lending money.

5. Don't just look at the upside

If your plan is too gushing about your prospects your bank may form the view that you are not looking at the proposition realistically. Perhaps they will consider you are too over-optimistic to be good in business.

Take one common issue: competition. If there is a lot of competition, state this clearly. Explain what the other places offer, and then explain in what ways you intend to offer something different and distinctive which will persuade some people to switch allegiance to you.

Don't give the impression that it will all be plain sailing – show the bank how you will address challenges.

6. Don't dismiss your business plan as just a formality

If you prepare your plan with care it will give you quite a good idea of the financial realities of running your own business. It will also bring home to you the responsibilities you will take on to your many suppliers and creditors, including of course HMRC. Perhaps you will be pleasantly surprised or at least reassured and encouraged to go on. Perhaps you will start to have second thoughts about the whole idea.

If you have serious doubts, it's far better to pull out at this stage, before you have taken on commitments which will be difficult and costly to get out of later.

Using an insurance broker

For any small business insurance is an important issue – don't skimp.

It's a pain having to pay out lots of money in insurance premiums when claims are so infrequent, but if you do have to make a claim you will kick yourself if your cover is inadequate. Remember also that an insurance company will expect you to meet your legal obligations in important areas such as employment law and health and safety (see Chapters Eight and Nine). You should carry out a risk assessment of your premises.

In the case of a sandwich-coffee bar the main risks to business premises come from:
- **Fires:** electrical faults are the biggest cause – check electrical items and wiring regularly – don't ignore that threadbare looking wire coming out of the contact grill.
- **Water Damage:** mainly caused by burst pipes and leaks from water tanks. Inspect regularly, especially when the temperature drops noticeably during the winter months.
- **Burglary:** give serious consideration to installing a burglar alarm – a very visible deterrent.
- **Employee injuries:** take precautions to guard against injuries. Ask your employees to tell you if they have any 'near misses'.

All employers must have Employer's Liability Insurance which, amongst other things, compensates employees who are injured or suffer illness as a result of working for you.

Why use an insurance broker? To save money and hassle

The cost of insurance can vary dramatically from company to company. In addition, insurance companies sometimes impose increases because they've sustained large claims in a particular year. Accordingly it may be in your interests to change companies from time to time. Add to this the fact that you may require a considerable range of insurances – motor, buildings, contents, business interruption, employer's liability and so on – and you can see that the assistance of an expert in the insurance field might well be a good idea.

A good insurance broker will assess your requirements, advise on the kind of insurance you should have and *not* try to get you to take out policies which you really don't need.

A broker will also review all your insurance policies on an annual basis and compare the renewal premiums being quoted by your present company with the rates currently being charged by competitors. In this way you can be assured that the premiums you are paying remain competitive.

You could, of course, do it yourself. But when you're busy running a sandwich-coffee bar you probably won't have time to undertake this kind of exercise. Your premiums will probably be paid by direct debit and you may well not register the fact that they have gone up considerably one year – or if you do, you may well put off doing anything about it and then forget all about it until the following year.

Bear in mind also that insurance brokers don't charge you anything for their service – they get their commission from the insurance company. They will also usually help with the paperwork involved in making claims should the need arise and this can be a real benefit for busy small-business people.

A few words of caution

Some brokers are tied to particular insurance companies and will be keen to sell *their* policies. It is most important that you choose a broker who is independent and whose only interest is to secure the right policy at the right price. The other worry I sometimes have is that once they've set up your policies it's more convenient for them just to see them renewed each year rather than put too much effort into seriously checking out the possibility of cheaper policies. So as the years go by you should keep an eye on the level of your premiums. Don't be afraid to challenge your broker if the premiums strike you as being on the high side.

As with other advisors you want someone who is familiar with small businesses – not all of them are. If you don't have an insurance broker at the present time then, as always, a personal recommendation from someone who is in business would be very valuable.

Insurance brokers are often financial consultants as well and might be able to help with personal investments, pensions and the arrangement of loans for business expansion or indeed house purchase.

Understanding the role of the environmental health officer

A cross between Dracula and the secret police?

This is how some people see environmental health officers (EHOs). It's really not like that. A great deal of what they have to say amounts to mere common sense. In general they are keen to get on with their job, which is to help you comply with the numerous statutory provisions affecting the food industry insofar as they apply to you. They have no interest in being gratuitously awkward.

> **Isn't it a good thing that there are officials ensuring that the risk of members of the public buying food which will give them food poisoning or worse is reduced as far as possible?**

There are many matters that fall within an EHO's area of responsibility. The main ones that affect you (which are dealt with in Chapter Nine) are these:

◆ cleaning schedules for the shop
◆ staff training in food hygiene
◆ temperature controls
◆ pest control records
◆ staff personal hygiene
◆ the decorative condition of the shop
◆ the general working system in the shop.

You might think that an EHO is someone you will only come across once you're up and running and this will certainly be true – if you wait for him to contact you. But in my view it is in your interests to take the initiative and make contact before you start trading and, crucially, before you commit yourself to a particular site. It is a good idea to regard the EHO as part of your initial team of advisors.

The point is that although you might think a particular unit is perfect for your needs there may be problems from an environmental health point of view – and you should know about them in advance.

Let's take a concrete example: is there a mechanical vent in the toilet? It's a legal requirement, not just for what might appear to be the obvious reason but also to remove chemical fumes associated with cleaning materials and the like. If there is no extractor in your chosen shop unit, is there a nearby flue through which air can be mechanically extracted by means of a pipe or duct? If not you might have to install ducting from the toilet to an exterior wall. What kind of distance is involved? Perhaps the ducting will have to be fitted under the floorboards. How long will it take? *How much will it all cost?*

You may, of course, find that there are no particular problems. This is all to the good; but you will almost certainly find that your EHO gives you some useful free advice for the future. When you arrange to meet your EHO, have a rough plan of your intended layout with the position of fridges, serve-over units, etc. so that the advice you receive is as well informed as possible.

A word of warning

If you are interested in acquiring a going concern and want to arrange a visit from the EHO prior to the conclusion of a deal you might encounter resistance from the current owners. It may be that they are doing something they shouldn't be doing. They want to sell their business so the last thing they want is any hassle from the authorities which might involve them in any expense. Don't let this put you off. Business is business, and it is very much in the interests of your fledgling business to have as much information as possible at this stage of the game. If a seller doesn't want to let an EHO into the shop you should immediately be suspicious and make it clear that if the seller is not prepared to allow such a visit you might have to reconsider your interest in the property.

It is true that some EHOs can be officious and a bit self-important on occasion. But in my experience most problems are caused by people not complying with the rules and then burying their heads in the sand when the breaches are spotted. The fact is that your local environmental health department has the right to inspect your premises, so you can't hide anything from them. They will usually find something wrong, however minor, but unless it is serious, you will be allowed a reasonable period of time to rectify matters.

> **SOUND ADVICE:** When setting up your sandwich bar it is a very good idea indeed to take the initiative and invite your EHO in at the earliest opportunity. Apart from anything else he will be impressed by your sensible attitude and will make a mental note that he probably won't have any difficulty in his dealings with you in future.

Getting help from a refrigeration advisor

Nowadays it would be unthinkable to open a sandwich bar which did not have good quality refrigeration units. You will probably require at least:

- a substantial open-fronted display (or dairy) unit for your sandwiches and salads. If space allows you will also be able to keep other items such as yoghurts and drinks in this unit.
- one good-sized serve-over or 'delicatessen unit' for your sandwich ingredients.
- a good quality industrial storage fridge.
- a commercial quality upright or chest freezer (space considerations will dictate which).

There are quite a lot of furnishings and pieces of equipment which can be acquired fairly late on in the proceedings. *Large refrigerated units are definitely not amongst them.* The problem is that it can take months from placing the order to having big units delivered. You can't open without them and it can be incredibly frustrating to find that everything is ready but you are prevented from opening because a crucial piece of the jigsaw is missing.

It is a good idea to make contact with experts in the field early on in your business planning.

Refrigeration experts can show you brochures, discuss capacity, delivery times, etc. and generally help you to decide on the right unit for your operation. If you have not dealt with the particular company before you might be asked to pay a deposit when you place your order.

Sudden unexpected closures are bad for business

Apart from delivery issues, a refrigeration expert is also of great importance after you have opened. If your serve-over unit breaks down at ten o'clock on a summer's morning it might affect your ability to trade if it's not fixed quickly. It's as serious as that. Regular customers will be forced to go elsewhere and might like what they find. Passers-by too will try somewhere else and might not try you again.

The point is that if you do experience a problem of this sort you need to have somebody reliable who can respond without delay and get you trading normally again. A refrigeration expert can also give advice on ways in which you can make your larger refrigerated units function most efficiently and also how to maintain them in order to ensure as long a life as possible.

One other point on this subject: if you are unlucky enough to suffer a power cut for a prolonged period of time and you lose refrigerated and frozen supplies as a result, get something in writing from your electricity supplier confirming the details – you will need this for any insurance claim.

> **A refrigeration expert is vital to the smooth running and economic well-being of your sandwich bar.**

Using shopfitters, decorators, plumbers and electricians

I shall deal later in the book with the issue of whether it is better for you to use a firm of shop-fitters or individual tradespeople to fit out the shop. In the meantime bear in mind that good tradespeople are very often booked weeks if not months in advance. For this reason, part of the process of concluding a deal should be to check that the particular people you have in mind will be available at the appropriate time to allow you to open on your preferred date. Don't assume that they are waiting around in their offices ready to spring into action when your call comes. It might not be a bad idea to have a second choice in mind in the event that your chosen person is unavailable because, for instance, they are held up on another job. Such eventualities are particularly likely in the case of smaller or one-person operations.

CHAPTER THREE

Choosing Your Shop Unit

What to look for in a particular area

Location is of course the most important consideration. No matter how tempting your sandwiches and coffee, most people won't travel far for their lunchtime food. They don't have time and there are so many desirable alternatives on offer these days. It's a buyer's market and you need to be where the buyers are.

You have to be confident that there are sufficient people within easy reach of your chosen unit to provide a sufficient level of business. In this respect sandwich-coffee bars are different from quality restaurants. It is remarkable the distances people will travel in order to experience the delights on offer from the latest top chef. It seems to be part of the fun. With restaurants it is possible to set up in a novel location and, through advertising and word of mouth recommendations, build up business. *This is not an option in the case of sandwich-coffee bars.*

> **Initial research is vital. You might know your town or city like the back of your hand – but now you must look at familiar places in a different way.**

Your aim is to build up a clear picture of the good locations – the hot spots. This way, when you are serious about proceeding and ready to view premises as they come on to the market, you will know the ones that are likely to be worth pursuing. Why spend lots of time looking at places that are no-hopers?

Drive to different areas of town at different times of day especially lunchtime. Park the car and observe the scene – particularly near established sandwich bars. Bear in mind that the lunchtime rush for take-away food can occur at different times in different parts of the town or city. You will need to spend a fair bit of time at each location.

When considering a particular location there a number of key factors to consider; some obvious, some less so.

1 Is it busy?

Do the pavements benefit from what a nearby competitor of mine memorably described as 'molten people'. Is the particular road an important artery which different groups of people have to use to walk from place to place? Will you thus have a captive audience? These are particularly important considerations for the passing trade element of your business.

2. Are there nearby offices?

The lunchtime office trade is an important factor for most sandwich-coffee bars in town and city centres. Remember people will not walk all that far for a sandwich, even a very good one. They might have as little as half an hour for lunch, so a few hundred yards can make a difference. The British climate can also make longer outings at lunch time hazardous affairs.

Do a bit of snooping around. You might discover the head office of a major company a short walk away. Great news! But if it has a good quality, heavily subsidised canteen it won't be much help to you (though people do often fancy a change and a breath of fresh air).

If you see a site being redeveloped check with the planning authority to find out what it's going to be and indeed whether they are aware of any other developments which might be happening in the near future in the area.

3. Are there some sandwich-coffee bars in the area already?

If not it is probably because there isn't enough business. Given the massive increase in the number of take-away food outlets in recent years in numerous locations it is unlikely that you will break into virgin territory. In general it's more important to go where the business is and compete with the existing operations on quality and new ideas. Having said that, if there are two or three established operations near your preferred site offering something very similar to what you have in mind you might well do better to look elsewhere. There's no point in saturating the market.

There is something of the law of the jungle about it all. At any time there are usually one or two weaker beasts in an area ready to be preyed upon and picked off. It may well be the case that a nearby owner has been at it for quite some time and is longing to retire to Spain. He may not be up to the idea of taking on a whole lot of new ideas in order to compete with thrusting incomers. You never know, it might be you one day....

4. How good are the logistics of travel, delivery and parking?

If you live on one side of town and your favoured location is on the other, how do you fancy the prospect of driving across town, quite possibly in busy traffic, simply to get to and from work every day? If you have children, what implications will this have for the school run?

It may be that you will choose to produce some food in your own home (see Chapter Six). Do you relish the thought of making a number of return journeys every day in order to deliver bacon, salmon, cakes or whatever might be needed for lunchtime? Bear in mind that such journeys often have to be made under pressure of time; and what if you realise half-way to the shop that you've forgotten something vital, or left the oven on?

On the subject of delivery, what are the parking restrictions? All major cities are struggling with the problems created by ever-increasing traffic. In some, draconian restrictions have been introduced. This can mean that delivery vehicles, no matter how determined, find it very difficult to stop at various times of the day – often the very times when you want them to deliver, in the morning or later in the afternoon.

Bear in mind also that if parking is severely restricted during the day then passing motorists will be deterred from making spur of the moment decisions to pull up outside your place, no matter how enticing you have made it.

> **Practical considerations are very important and merit hard-headed consideration. It's all too easy to overlook them in the heat of the moment when you are viewing a property and get carried away by its wonderfully elegant proportions! If you do this you might well live to regret it.**

5. Location, location, location – think outside the box

From the first four points it will be clear that what you are looking for is a place where the action is, where the demand is and which is easy to get at. The trouble is this means you will be competing with other people for what are regarded conventionally as the best spots. It may well be unavoidable but it will mean that a lot of your precious start-up capital will go on simply securing your site. Sometimes a bit of lateral thinking can demonstrate the potential of places which on the face of it don't quite achieve these ideal criteria.

Sandwich-coffee bars have, in recent times, opened in parts of towns and cities where previously they would not have been commercially viable; in neighbourhoods where in the past there was probably just the odd small baker's shop or deli with a sandwich sideline. This has come about because of the general increase in demand for good quality food outlets, which has spread out from the town and city centres. So don't think only of the obvious places: consider areas a bit further away from the centre. See if new ventures have started up and assess whether they appear to be thriving. *Try to be a bit ahead of the game.*

In addition, consider places which are near the best locations but perhaps a little way down a side street or even up a flight of stairs. If you can make a unit in such a location clearly visible from the street and if going there will only involve a customer in a very short, easy detour then you may get the best of both worlds: a cheaper property in a commercially viable location. It can also mean that obtaining permission for, say, restaurant use, is easier because there are not a lot of similar places in the immediate vicinity. *Obtaining such permission can, of course, add to the value of your investment.*

Our second shop was in just such a 'yes but' location. I was aware of it being on the market for several months before I actually bothered to go and see it. Even then I reckoned it was not quite right. It is in what might be called a tertiary trading location two miles from the city centre. It is not even in the main trading thoroughfare for the area.

My wife pointed out, however, that although it was a short distance from the commercial heart of the area its frontage projected from the shop next door – only by a foot or so but enough to provide space for a sign which would be clearly visible from the main road. Not only that but, although the unit was one of only two units in this particular road, it was something of an arterial route; parking was easy and the pavement was wide enough to allow some tables and chairs outside.

In the event we were the only people seriously interested and were able to buy the property at a favourable price.

This story illustrates another important point:

Even if a property is not in the very best of locations it can nonetheless do well for reasons specific to the particular area.

The shop is situated quite close to the main university halls of residence. In addition there are quite a few student flats nearby and our shop is situated on a road which many students use to go to and from the main campuses in the city. Students seem to like the kind of things we do and so we have built up a very strong following indeed from amongst their ranks. You could find similar situations with schools, large out of town office complexes or sites associated with tourists.

Beware – there are also drawbacks associated with such locations

There can be times of the year (in our case the student vacations) when you suddenly find that business drops off markedly. This can be extremely disconcerting to begin with. It really takes a full year of trading to get to know the patterns. This is important because it prepares you for the sudden changes which can cause staffing and cash flow problems.

If you do decide to aim your appeal mainly at one particular group do make sure that your particular way of doing things is likely to appeal to them. Please excuse the sweeping generalisations but plain cheese sandwiches will not go down well with reasonably affluent students and sushi is unlikely to be the number one choice for people working on a building site.

There is another potential problem. The available market will inevitably be more limited than that in the city centre. If another switched-on operation moves into a nearby unit you could find that your turnover is quite badly affected – all year round.

Is market research appropriate?

Most large organisations would not consider opening a new outlet without first carrying out sophisticated market research at considerable expense. The purpose is to check market viability and, of course, that people actually want what you are going to be selling. If you wish to test the market directly it is unlikely your resources will stretch to this.

Asking your prospective customers

You will have to rely on your own ability to get information out of people in the area in order to assess the strength of the market. This is not for the faint of heart as it will involve approaching people in local offices and shops as well as people in the street. You might ask them:

◆ how often they buy food to take away at lunchtime
◆ what sort of things they buy at present
◆ what sort of new things they would like to be able to buy at lunchtime
◆ how long they can be away from the office

◆ how much they are prepared to spend
◆ whether it is important for them to be able to sit in
◆ any other questions which you regard as useful for the particular kind of operation you have in mind.

I must be honest and confess that although I did think about this before we opened our first shop I did not do it. I had lived in Edinburgh for 20 years and knew the city well. I simply relied on the other types of research detailed earlier. It's difficult to say with certainty that such market research will be productive, but you've nothing to lose (except some of your precious time).

What's more, you might just pick up a few comments which could avoid wasting effort on some treasured idea – and maybe even gain a slight edge over the competition. And if you include your findings in your business plan your bank will be very impressed.

There are two situations in which I think some form of detailed market research would be advisable:

◆ If you are new to an area. In this case there is a real possibility of going for the wrong place and finding out the hard way that it's not going to work.
◆ If you decide to do a bit of empire building and open another outlet in a town or city with which you are not particularly familiar.

Help from other sources

There is a range of help available to assist you with market research. In the first place there will be local, publicly funded organisations set up to help and encourage small business start-ups. They will be able to give general information and profiles of cities and towns. They will come under the heading 'Business Link' ('Small Business Gateway' in Scotland and 'Business Connect' in Wales). See Chapter One for phone numbers. Once you have decided on a particular area or areas, in the bigger cities, they can refer you to local enterprise or development companies which can give more specialised information about particular locations. These services are all free. If you have any problems making contact simply phone your local council who will be able to help.

In addition you should speak to local estate agents specialising in small commercial properties and businesses. Remember though that whilst they will doubtless have the benefit of good local knowledge they will also be keen to dispose of particular properties on behalf of their clients.

Finally, if you really want to get under the skin of particular areas you can instruct a professional firm of market researchers to carry out a survey on your behalf. Needless to say such a service will not come cheap. You should check the *Yellow Pages* and speak to a number of firms in order to satisfy yourself that the service they provide is one you need.

Don't forget though: the most important element of all is your gut instinct.

Purchase or lease?

It's really a question of money. If you can afford it I'm not in any doubt that it's best to buy a property. You acquire an investment which maintains and hopefully increases its value in real terms; and because you are trading from it you know it's being properly looked after. In years to come, when you decide to call it a day, you have a valuable asset which you can then let out. In due course you can sell it and enhance the quality of your retirement. However, this is all easier said than done because:

- ◆ **In the best locations it is hard to acquire property.** Many owners prefer to hang onto the asset. This means that property to purchase is hard to come by and often commands a premium price.
- ◆ **By no means everybody can afford it.** Commercial loans usually involve larger deposits than private house purchases. Add this to the cost of acquiring a business and/or buying a lot of new equipment and it's not hard to see that renting is the realistic option for many people. You also have to have the income to justify the loan. If you have a mortgage already then this may be difficult.

Bear in mind also that property purchase is not all straightforward.

If in due course, you let the property out, you might experience hassle with tenants. The most common and irritating of such problems is late or non-payment of rent. If you have bought a property in a location away from the most desirable central areas you might find that by the time you come to sell, property in that part of the world is not in great demand. You could then be left with something of a white elephant which involves you in ongoing advertising costs, compulsory repairs and general worry. This is something of a worst case scenario, however, and I do think that if you can afford it, purchase is best.

The renting option

However, if purchase is not an option it's most definitely not the end of the world. Renting is the chosen route for many people who start out in business and it has the obvious advantage that you don't need to find a substantial deposit from your own resources. Your available finances can be concentrated on fitting out the shop the way you want it. In addition, you will probably find that you have more properties to choose from.

> **Renting allows you to start up in business with the smallest possible initial outlay.**

It might also be possible to have an option to purchase written into the lease which could become exerciseable, say, at the first rent review. If the owner is agreeable to this then you have the advantage that you don't have to compete for the property on the open market. The usual provision is that the price payable will be open market value. There will, of course, be room for debate as to what constitutes open market value at any given time but with reasonableness on both sides this should not be a major problem.

Landlords sometimes prefer small independents as tenants. Unlike bigger companies which are often inflexible about details and have to go through time-consuming meetings at different levels to arrive at decisions, small independents can make quick decisions. They are also flexible enough to fit in with landlord's aspirations for a particular site.

A landlord will want to be assured that you will responsibly meet the tenant's obligations under the lease. You might be required to produce a CV or business plan to reassure the landlord. It will be for you to decide if such requests are reasonable in particular circumstances.

There are a number of points to bear in mind when leasing:

◆ In particularly desirable locations you may have to pay a premium – what in some parts of the world is referred to as 'key money'. This is simply the purchase price payable for the existing lease of the premises which reflects the demand for a particular property at a particular time – and it can work both ways. When the commercial property market was in the doldrums some years ago it was not uncommon to see properties advertised for rent with 'incentives available' or 'reverse premiums' – i.e. the incoming tenant was offered a payment simply as an inducement to take on a lease.

◆ It is vital that you are aware of the terms of the lease and that they are reasonably fair to you. Needless to say this must be sorted out right at the start. Once you've committed yourself to the lease you can't complain later when you discover that it contains some terms which are not favourable to you. This harks back to the importance of engaging a solicitor experienced in this kind of work – and getting them involved as early in the proceedings as possible.

◆ If your business fails and ceases trading it is up to you to find a new tenant or sub-tenant. You have to keep on paying rent until you do and this could, of course, be a considerable burden.

◆ If you own a property there is a good chance that its value will increase over the years. In the case of rented property you have to hope that the goodwill of the business you create will acquire a value which you will be able to realise in the future. However, goodwill is a far less certain asset than bricks and mortar.

Getting to know the property

A general point that applies to all properties, bought or rented, is that you should find out as much as you can about any matters which might adversely affect you.

◆ Is another sandwich bar or café about to open next door?
◆ Have there been recent problems with the roof?
◆ Has the local authority made a recent order for essential repairs to the property? If so, it won't be your financial responsibility, but the works might, for instance, lead to the cordoning off of adjacent pavements which could be bad for business.
◆ Are there problem neighbours?
◆ Have there been break-ins to the property or surrounding shops?
◆ Are any of the adjoining properties unoccupied and thus a possible route in for burglars?

The point is that people trying to dispose of properties and/or businesses don't want to tell you things which might put you off, which is understandable. You should, therefore, find out as much as possible about the property, good and bad, before committing yourself to it. I'm not saying that difficulties concerning the points mentioned above will necessarily mean that you should not pursue an interest in a property, but they should be taken into account.

> **Your aim should ideally be to know as much about the property as the current owner or tenant so that you can make a fully informed decision on whether to proceed. Don't hesitate to snoop around a bit and ask questions of neighbouring proprietors. Speak to your solicitor and surveyor; they might have invaluable local knowledge.**

Empty unit or going concern?

There are advantages and disadvantages with both options.

Taking on an empty unit

If you take on an empty or shell unit you are obviously going to have to do the place up from scratch. This will mean a lot of time and expense. If there are old, economically worthless fittings and wiring and plumbing systems in the place then these will all have to be stripped out. Having incurred expenditure to acquire the place you will now have to spend more money and wait some time – possibly months – before you see the money starting to flow the other way. On the other hand, of course, you will not have had to pay for goodwill, fittings, fixtures or equipment.

There are other distinct advantages:

◆ The process of acquiring the place should be more straightforward. You are only going to be negotiating over the value of the property or the appropriate level of rent.
◆ You have a blank sheet on which to impose your vision without hindrance.
◆ Electrical and plumbing work will be much more straightforward – your tradespeople won't have to work under and round units.
◆ You (and more importantly your surveyor) can have a really good look at the fabric of the property in advance. This way you are less likely to come across nasty surprises when you get into the place and start work.
◆ When everything is completed you can be confident that the work has been done the way you want it. And if there are any problems you know whose door to knock on to get them sorted out.

Taking on a going concern

If you take over a going concern the main advantage is that you can get trading quickly. No doubt you will want to redecorate and introduce other changes in order to stamp your own particular style on the place, but with a bit of forward planning it shouldn't take long. You don't have to be involved with so many tradespeople and you don't have to worry about delivery times for serve-over units and the like. However, there are a number of potential difficulties to bear in mind:

1. Valuing the business

The problem of dealing with a small-businessperson! The value of a business relates to how much profit you the purchaser can make from it taking into account the risks and costs involved. Past profitability and asset values are important but are not the whole story.

Assuming the business you want to buy has been built up over a number of years, the owners may well have an inflated idea of what the business is worth. They may see this as the big pay-off after years of hard work – an emotional element. So in addition to the fairly straightforward business of agreeing a figure for the property (purchase price or rental), you have to negotiate figures for goodwill, fittings and fixtures, stock and equipment with the person or people whose life's work they might represent. If recent profit levels are unimpressive you may well be told, 'Of course the trading accounts don't tell the whole story.' In other words the seller doesn't declare all their earnings. If you come up against this, simply point out that all you can go on is what is shown in the accounts.

Sometimes the negotiations can revolve around a global figure, but to arrive at this you have to value the individual components which go to make up the figure. This can involve professionals such as accountants, which, of course, adds to the expense.

You may not want to buy all items of stock or equipment. The sellers will probably resist this because second-hand catering equipment and old packets of crisps will not be much use to them and will be of little value.

In my experience such negotiations can be lengthy and tedious.

And what does goodwill really mean? It is particularly hard to work out in the case of small businesses. You will hear advisors talking about 'the amount by which the going concern value exceeds the asset value' or 'what you pay for making a profit above your time and investment of capital'. But there are so many uncertainties. Will the previous loyal customers automatically come to you? If you do things differently they might not.

There might also have been a strong personal following for the previous owner.

I think arguments about the value of the goodwill of small independent businesses like sandwich-coffee bars are especially weak nowadays when there are so many places to choose from, often in close proximity. *Particularly since far and away the most important factor in your success will be your own hard work and imagination.* Then again, if you happen to be in an area where there are not many comparable places and where planning permission for what you want to do is hard to come by, then this would inflate the level of goodwill a seller could reasonably expect to achieve.

At the end of the day you have to work out what a business is worth to you and negotiate hard. Needless to say, if there is a forced sale situation, e.g. because a seller is unwell, you will be in a much stronger position.

> **The true value of a business is the price a seller and buyer are prepared to agree.**

My wife and I started both of our sandwich bars from shell units – and we had an established customer base within weeks both times.

2. Taking on existing employees

When a business changes hands, employees of the previous owner automatically become employees of the new employer on the same terms and conditions as before. It is as if their contracts of employment had originally been made with the new employer. Thus employees' continuity of employment is preserved, as are their terms and conditions of employment under their contracts of employment. Now, what you have in mind for the business might be different from the previous owner – also you might not be so keen on the young guy with the ring through his nose or the old lady who insists on smoking outside the front door. But if you decide to get rid of them you could find yourself on the receiving end of a claim for unfair dismissal.

For more information on this you should obtain a booklet called 'Employment Rights on the Transfer of an Undertaking' (PL 699 Rev 4). This can be obtained from your nearest Jobcentre. See also Chapter Nine which deals with employment matters.

3. Equipment

Assuming you do come to an agreement you will end up with at least some equipment which is old and out of guarantee. Will it let you down? Possibly. Is it really worth much? No. Is it state of the art? Probably not. You get the picture?

4. Decorating

It's not so easy to get the place looking the way you want it. Previous regular customers will be able to tell that the old place has simply had a bit of a facelift – and they might not be much impressed.

5. Complying with regulations

Does the unit comply with current food hygiene and health and safety rules and regulations? Will you have to spend money to bring it up to the necessary standards? As mentioned previously it is advisable to get an EHO or other expert to look over a place before you are committed to it. For all you know the owner is selling because he has been told he has to make costly changes or face the possibility of closure. Don't find yourself unwittingly picking up the tab for this. It is possible that a lender will wish to be assured that the premises have been checked by an expert for any such potential pitfalls.

Making a choice

The difficulty with all such considerations is that you will have to make your choice from the range of properties that happens to come on to the market when you are looking for a place. You may have weeks of waiting and fruitless viewing sessions before the right place comes along. It's not a perfect world and you will doubtless end up having to make compromises.

> **The best you can do is weigh up the pros and cons of a particular place, speak to your advisers and then follow your instinct.**

What to look for in a particular shop unit

Now that you have:
◆ selected and primed your team of professional and other advisers
◆ selected a location with potential
◆ decided on your preferred basis for acquiring a property

… it's time to start considering specific units. It will be unlikely that the first one you see is the right one for you. Besides, it's a sound idea to look at as many places as possible so that you can make comparisons and get a feel for what kind of unit best fits in with your ideas. Make sure you get to know about all properties which are available at any given time.

◆ **Make yourself aware of any new places as they come onto the market.** Check all publications that advertise property. Make sure you get hold of them on the day they come out. Always try to be ahead of the field.

◆ **Register with property agents who specialise in small to medium-sized commercial units and the sale of businesses.** You will almost certainly be bombarded with lots of unsuitable material – but you can use it as scrap paper for making lists and drawing endless internal plans of the shop. Think commercial.

◆ **Keep your eyes peeled when you're out and about driving.** Make a point of driving around the hot spots on a regular basis. You might see a sign before the unit is actually advertised in the press, thus allowing you to get in early.

◆ **Approach the proprietors of suitable units even though they are not being advertised.** This applies to any unit that might be suitable, not just ones which are trading as take-away food outlets. It does require a bit of brass neck, I know, but it can pay off. I acquired a small office in Edinburgh in this way in 1979 and sold it a few years ago for a large profit.

◆ **Check out empty units which look as if they might be suitable and approach your local rating office.** Obtain details of the owners and try to make contact to see if they would be interested in disposing of the property. It is a very long shot but what have you got to lose? Your solicitor will be able to help with this if necessary.

I have a hunch that there may be one other source of properties in good locations in years to come. There has been a rapid expansion of sandwich-coffee bars in recent years by the big chains. I suspect some may have overstretched themselves. One such sandwich-coffee bar in a prime location in Edinburgh ceased trading after a short time. The unit was advertised to let for quite some time. It was eventually acquired by a local operator who, I suspect, picked it up for a good price. It would not surprise me if this phenomenon becomes more common; and the fact that one of the big chains couldn't make a go of it would not mean that an imaginative independent operation could not do better.

Knowing what to look for

By the time you come to view properties you should have a fairly clear idea of what you are looking for. There are a number of important matters to keep in mind:

Is it big enough for what you want to do?

It may seem an obvious point, but if you see a place which is strong on location and price it can be tempting to try to 'fit a quart into a pint pot'. Take a tape measure and get the vital statistics. When you get home make a scale drawing and cut out bits of paper to scale to represent work-top areas, fridges, freezers, tables and chairs. Play around with everything to see how it all goes together. When doing this always remember the following points:

◆ Make sure you allow sufficient space for customers to circulate and staff to move about without getting in each other's way. There are regulations regarding the minimum width of corridors etc. Your EHO will give you advice on such matters.

◆ Assuming you have an internal seating area, be sure that your massive (you hope) lunchtime queue is not going to interfere with those customers peacefully reading the paper over their cappuccinos.

◆ You obviously hope that the venture will succeed, so make allowance also for the possibility of some expansion – another refrigerated sandwich display unit, some more chairs.

Modify your plans by all means, but if it is clear that it won't work there really is no point in pursuing it, no matter how appealing the property is in other ways.

If you intend to set up a small to medium-sized operation then as a general guide a unit of between 500 and 900 square feet (45 and 85 square metres) should allow you to trade efficiently. Approximately 60% of the space will be given over to public areas: display units, tables and chairs, bar and stools and the 'milling around' area. The rest will be taken up by the food preparation area, office or office area, and toilet. This size may not seem very big but in fact the public often prefer a cosy, busy-feeling place to one which has empty spaces.

Is there room on the pavement for tables and chairs?

Although you may think the British weather makes this irrelevant, after years of holidays abroad people here are keener than ever on many aspects of foreign culture. Sitting outside chatting to their friends over a fruit smoothie, or simply people-watching, are high up the list.

Even if you can't change the weather it is now possible to create a more customer-friendly atmosphere outside. You can buy sturdy and substantial umbrellas which cover large areas and look attractive. In addition you can buy patio heaters, fuelled by calor gas, which are remarkably effective and can allow people to sit outside in comfort even on cooler days. (They are less effective if it is windy.) All these things, plus tables and chairs, can be purchased at reasonable cost from any good-sized garden centre.

Cordon off the seating area with a few plant pots and you can create an attractive outward impression of your sandwich-coffee bar, which in itself creates interest and advertises the place.

> **Do remember to ensure that you or your staff clear the tables regularly.**
> **When you're working hard inside the shop it's easy to forget about what's**
> **happening outside – and dirty tables give a very bad impression to the public.**

Another point to bear in mind is that you will require permission from your local authority. They will carry out an inspection. They will only give permission if they are satisfied that there is sufficient room for pedestrians and wheelchair users to pass the tables and chairs with ease. They will doubtless charge a fee; in Edinburgh the initial fee is currently £75 with an annual renewal fee of £25. Permission will be granted subject to certain conditions such as a prohibition against playing music. In addition, sitting outside will probably be limited to particular hours of the day (in Edinburgh currently 10.30am until 9.00pm) and times of the year (in Edinburgh currently April until October).

Does the unit benefit from good security?
Sandwich-coffee bars don't tend to be popular targets for people looking for money. Apart from during trading hours there really isn't much of ready value on the premises (assuming you don't sell cigarettes or alcohol). However, it is a depressing fact that any shop unit can be a target for burglars and vandals. If your shop is vandalized or burgled, it can be expensive, inconvenient and demoralising, so you should reduce the risk as far as possible. Bear in mind these points:

◆ If the shop is in an isolated position it is more likely to experience problems. In general, if a shop is part of a well-lit block with adjacent shops and flats above it is less likely to be a target. There are more people around, especially at night.
◆ If there are empty or derelict properties close to the shop these can provide routes into your shop for the more determined criminal.
◆ Does the shop have a security system and/or a roller shutter? If not, these may well be items you have to consider when making a list of outlays in your business plan.

◆ If most of the flats or houses around a shop have alarm systems this may well mean it is an area which experiences problems.

◆ If the shop is situated close to pubs or nightclubs this can be problem, not during the day, but late at night when the revellers emerge, often the worse for drink.

◆ If it is next door to an off-licence it might possibly used as a route into the off-licence.

◆ You might be very attracted by a unit with large old-fashioned front windows, especially if they have an elegant curve or two. Beware. If a window like this is smashed it can be horribly expensive to repair. It might involve ordering glass specially so that you are left for weeks with a partly boarded up frontage. Your insurance company may then increase your premiums or try to get you to put in different windows which would be less expensive to repair.

> **And something to remember when you're up and running: always empty the till at night and leave the drawer open – *if possible so that it is visible from outside*. You will discourage opportunist thieves since there will be little else of interest to them. Also bear in mind that your insurance company may well not pay out for damage to a till not left open at night in this way.**

Go back and look at the place on several occasions

I mentioned hard-headedness before; it's essential when viewing properties. You want to set up your own business. You're in love with the idea. Watch out, because this is the time when common sense can be squeezed out of the picture by over-enthusiasm.

   View the place at least three times. Get to the know the owner. As I mentioned previously it's important to find out as much as you can – and the owner is the person who knows the answers. Ask them lots of questions. Ask yourself lots of questions. Visit at different times of day. Stand back. Talk to your solicitor and/or surveyor. Bounce thoughts and ideas off your partner. Don't take ages but make sure you've considered all aspects of the place before you take the plunge.

> **A thought to bear in mind: if you realise that you are agonising about a place and finding it really difficult to make a decision that is probably because deep down you don't think it's right for you; in which case it probably isn't.**

CHAPTER FOUR

Creating Your Own Identity

It's what a former American president called the 'vision thing'. You must have a good idea in your mind of what your sandwich-coffee bar is going to be like – what a customer walking into the place in a few months' time will experience.

Of course you can't possibly know every last detail in advance. You will inevitably make changes and additions as you go along – before and after opening – but it's important to have your own identity. This will serve to mark you out in the eyes of customers.

'Oh yes that's the place that does really good chicken sandwiches – classy' or 'I love the decor in that new place, really nice colours – the owners have obviously got good taste', or 'Curried parsnip and apple soup! They're welcome to it. It's not my cup of tea.'

Your identity will also give you a reference point which will help to guide you as you make decisions on a whole range of issues before you open. If you're not sure about something your identity will help to answer the question: 'Is that the sort of thing a place like ours would/should/could do?'

In this chapter I will discuss many of the elements which, taken together, go to make up the particular identity and character of a venture. The list is not exhaustive.

Choosing a name

Let's face it, people are not going to buy a sandwich from your establishment just because it's got a really impressive name. It's the quality of the sandwich which makes a name memorable not the other way round. If my school rock group had been called Led Zeppelin it still wouldn't have secured a recording contract!

A name is still important, though. There are a number of points to bear in mind.

A name should be easy to say, spell and memorise.

Your aim is to quickly become an established part of customers' daily lives and awareness. This is easier to achieve if your name is straightforward.

Your name will be used many times every day by a variety of suppliers, tradespeople and officials. It's very tedious if, repeatedly and routinely, you have to clarify the details or spelling of your trading name.

> When we were at the planning stage we considered a variety of names. We were confident that our trademark would be the well above-average quality of our food. This made us think French. I spoke to a French friend who suggested various names including 'Le Pain De Mie'. It makes me shudder to think of it now. Customers would have struggled with the pronunciation and business contacts would have struggled with the spelling.

A name should not tie you down to a particular concept.

Another name we thought of was 'La Baguette'. Not bad. However, as we thought about it more, it dawned on us that we would be selling a variety of breads, not just baguettes. Not only that, but for all we knew baguettes would go out of fashion in years to come; or perhaps we might decide to become purely a coffee shop. We might find ourselves having to change our name after years of trading – a waste of time and money – and confusing for customers.

A name should be decided on sooner rather than later.

Long before you sell your first sandwich there are people and organisations which will ask you for your trading name. The information is necessary when setting up accounts with suppliers and other business contacts.

> When we were considering the name 'La Baguette' we were in the process of acquiring our first shop. There was no telephone. When ordering a line BT wanted to know our name as it would appear in the phone book. I said I thought it might be 'La Baguette'. I wish I hadn't. Although I said it wasn't definite and although I wrote quite soon afterwards to tell them that in fact we would be called 'Millers' it made no difference. Our name appeared in the telephone book and on telephone bills as 'La Baguette' for about a year. This is typical of dealings with large organisations. Like strict quizmasters, it seems they have to take your first answer.

A name should not be overly clever or clichéd.

Making some kind of a neat joke out of your name is short-sighted. Jokes are only funny for a very short time. After that they are tedious or downright naff.

Equally, do you really want to be just another 'Coffee Pot' or 'Dave's Sandwich Bar'? Names like this are hardly going to help you stand out from what is a crowded field. In our own case 'Millers' became the clear favourite. I think it was a good choice; apart from anything else it happens to be a good 'bready' name for a sandwich bar. The worst that happens is that people spell it with an 'a' instead of an 'e' – a mild irritation but nothing more.

One of the most ill-judged names I have come across was provided by a sandwich-coffee bar located near our second shop. It was called 'The Renaissance Of Food.' In reality it was a very ordinary take-away. Apart from being pretentious and inaccurate the name was a real mouthful – far too long. Not long after we opened it closed.

Having said all this, one of the most successful sandwich-coffee bar chains of recent times has been 'Pret A Manger.' However, in much of their advertising they now appear to have dropped the 'A Manger' – presumably in the interests of simplicity.

Obviously there is a balance to be struck. There may be local, geographical or personal considerations which will influence you in favour of a particular name in your own case.

Keep your name straightforward and memorable and don't leave it late.
Don't forget – the sandwich-coffee bar makes the name not the other way round.

Creating a logo

When you have decided on a name it makes sense to create a logo. This could be a picture of some sort or your name in a particular style of print – or a combination of the two. You want to make yourself as visible as possible so it's a good idea to have the logo appear in as many places as possible, including:

- **Exterior signs:** projecting and/or on the windows/doors. I particularly like banner signs. Don't forget that you may well require local authority permission for projecting and banner signs.
- **Carrier bags:** you can have your logo printed onto the sides of small carrier bags – usually brown or white paper. This does add very slightly to the cost of each transaction, but wouldn't you like to see lots of people walking around advertising your sandwich bar? Don't give them out for people merely buying a bag of crisps and a can of juice.
- **Labels:** similarly, a form of advertising. The labels I have in mind are sticky labels which are used to seal each sandwich bag – so they're practical too. They come in rolls and are easily dispensed from strategically placed toilet roll holders.

    With carrier bags and labels you will, of course, need to engage the services of a printer. There is an initial outlay for the necessary artwork before the printing can begin.
- **Your car or van:** this is increasingly popular and obviously helps to raise your profile. However, if you are not going to buy a vehicle specifically for the shop you have to ask yourself if you want logos plastered all over your car.
- **Internal mirrors, menus, blinds, napkins and fitted entrance doormats:** I especially like fitted doormats with a logo woven into the fabric. It seems to me this helps to create a professional and well-established air for the customer on entry – and first impressions do count.
- **Staff aprons:** this really does help to create a professional, unified image. Definitely a good investment; but remember aprons should never be worn for more than one day before being washed.
- **Headed paper:** yes you should have headed paper! It looks professional and you will find many situations when it comes in handy: correspondence with your bank, responding to matters raised by the Environmental Health Department and simple matters such as sending off an adjusted payment following a phone call. It is a simple matter to set up a template of your headed paper in your word-processor. If you want you can print off some blank copies and then handwrite your message. Alternatively you can make it look a bit more businesslike by printing the whole letter.

A tip: when setting up your headed paper make it A5 size. It's reasonably small and can double as a compliments slip which is all you will need for a lot of routine communications.

> **You may be a small player in the business world but nowadays people are accustomed to and expect a corporate image which a logo helps to create.**

An artistic theme

There's no doubt that the quality of the food is paramount, but we live in a highly image-fashion-conscious age – *and people do expect to be impressed by the cover as well as the book.*

Clearly you will wish to choose pleasing colours inside and out, but what are you going to put on the walls? You could go to a print shop and buy copies of a few Impressionist paintings. However, decent-sized prints are surprisingly expensive and the idea is hardly very original; and they soon become dog-eared.

> **This is an area where you can and should give free rein to your imagination**
> **– dare to be different.**

Here are a few suggestions, some of which have been used in my shops and which have been favourably commented on.

1. Select one or more attractive paintings which you think would add to the character of your shop. Contact your nearest art college. Commission a student to do a copy to a scale that will fit in with the available space. You will probably find that the student's fee is very reasonable. In return you get a real painting (which you can hang in your living room when you decide to retire). *There might also be the prospect of a sideline here*: the student could advertise his or her services as a copyist and pay you a percentage of any fees for work thus obtained.

A word of warning: make sure you get a good look at some of the artist's work in advance, before you are committed, to ensure it will be of a good standard. If possible, try to get a look at the work as it progresses.

2. Allocate one wall as an exhibiting area for art students or local artists. You will have to agree what percentage of the price you will take and how long paintings should stay up before being replaced. The idea is that you have a point of interest to distract your lengthy lunchtime queues and discourage them from checking out the opposition. *Again, make sure you see paintings in advance – you don't want to end up with something inappropriate on the walls.*

3. Commission an art student to build a life-size figure which can be placed just outside the shop or in a strategic position inside. We did this for our second shop – a sinister looking man in a light brown coat. He has a bowler hat and wears dark sunglasses. He has become a local point of interest. More than once I have seen people stop (often at the behest of arm-yanking children) look at him, then come into the shop to buy something. **But do warn people making early morning deliveries.** I know of one case where a new bread delivery man almost had cardiac arrest when he unlocked the door and unexpectedly came face to face with our man!

4. You could also get an artist to create a huge mural covering one entire wall. Again, make sure you see and approve of the artist's ideas before going ahead.

A word of caution: if you do deal with art students be careful – in my experience whilst they are usually very pleasant, creative and stimulating people they don't always have good business heads. Deadlines and time limits don't always mean much to them. Only give them a deposit for materials upfront. Keep in touch on a regular basis to make sure they come up with the goods when you need them.

5. Allocate a space near the door where people can put up posters advertising forthcoming local events. Such posters are often colourful and interesting and help to give a lively impression to the shop. Here are some dos and don'ts:

◆ Don't allow people to put up any kind of political posters.
◆ Don't allow people to put up posters anywhere other than in the allocated area.
◆ Don't allow people to advertise rooms in flats, professional services, etc. – such notices have no artistic merit and if anything detract from the favourable impression you are trying to create.
◆ Do take posters down once the event advertised has happened.
◆ Do immediately remove any posters which people put up without asking permission first – they'll soon get the message.
◆ Do ask people advertising shows if you or your staff can have some complimentary tickets. Why not? You're giving them free advertising. I was once given over £60 worth of tickets for a circus during the Edinburgh Festival a few years ago.

6. Try to find a shop which sells old photographs of your town or city, and if possible of your neighbourhood. Buy a selection and put them in frames individually or in groups. It's a good idea to screw them to the wall – they won't go lopsided and they won't be removed by a light-fingered customer. You might think about turning this into a sideline by putting up a card with the shop's details and taking an agreed cut of any sales that result.

7. Display plants and cut flowers – they invariably add a touch of class. But make sure they are kept in good condition by regular watering or replacement. There is nothing worse than dead or dying plants or flowers. Many customers will see them as symptomatic of the state of the business.

If you don't want the hassle of maintaining them, it's probably best not to bother with them in the first place. Alternatively, engage a company (often associated with florists) who will provide and maintain plants and flowers and hanging baskets. *However, do you really want to spend some of your hard-earned money on something you should be able to take care of yourself?*

None of these ideas is expensive. If done well they can all add to the individual character of your sandwich-coffee bar and create a favourable impression for customers.

Using professionals to help you produce an image

There are many professional designers in a variety of fields who will be only too happy to give you advice and ideas on how to create a co-ordinated image for your sandwich-coffee bar. The trick is to get them really tuned in to what you are about. If you can do this then there is no doubt they have the ability to create an eye-catching image which at the same time tells people about the essence of your establishment.

However, their services do not come cheap. You have to ask yourself whether they are appropriate for a business the size of a small independent sandwich-coffee bar. Another related problem, one which I mentioned previously, is that many designers prefer bigger, more lucrative customers.

Ask yourself: don't you think that part of the fun of setting up a business is attending to things like this yourself? Perhaps the time to use them is later when you're established and want to give your unit a makeover or when you want to open another outlet and your 'corporate' image is more important.

If you think designers might be right for what you have in mind, speak to a few and ask them for some ideas on a no-obligation basis. You will see lots of them in the *Yellow Pages*. You will quickly know if they are right for you.

> If you do, I hope you have more luck than I did. My wife and I asked a firm of designers to give us the benefit of their professional experience and wisdom. A few days after our meeting, when we had explained that we were all about good quality food and tasteful surroundings, we received some very professionally prepared drawings. Unfortunately, what they showed was a picture of a fat cartoon-style pig guzzling some indeterminate brightly coloured concoction. The beast was slavering profusely. Accompanying this garish image was the unforgettable call to 'come and make a pig of yourselves at Millers'. When one of the designers phoned a few days later to see what I thought of his efforts we did not have a long conversation.

Creating and displaying signs

Signs serve two purposes: to attract attention and to provide information. They can also say a lot about you.

Exterior signs:
◆ permanent projecting signs
◆ banner signs (a length of sturdy material stretched between two projecting bars with your name or other information written in large lettering)
◆ sandwich blackboards
◆ wall-hanging blackboards
◆ lettering – including large individual plastic letters and plastic boards with your name and other details written on
◆ lettering – often contained within frosted glass effect plastic – which is stuck on windows in one sheet
◆ signs written or painted on the external walls
◆ free-standing metal signs provided by companies which advertise their products such as ice-cream or coffee
◆ neon signs
◆ a framed menu
◆ photographs of your products in internally lit display units.

Consider them all, but remember: whilst what they actually say is important, their most important purpose is to tell people that you are there and that you are open for business. Avoid clutter.

You might well need local authority permission for projecting and banner signs, especially if your building is listed or in a conservation area. So far as placing the freestanding signs on the pavement is concerned, my understanding is that in general a local authority will not object – so long as they don't receive any complaints. Use common sense (vital for all small business people – if you don't have any, go and get some right away) and make sure that any such signs don't cause any kind of obstruction.

Some sandwich-coffee bars exhibit photographs of the kinds of things available inside, sometimes in internally lit display boxes which are visible from outside. If done professionally I suppose this can look quite good. However, I wonder if this sort of image isn't more associated with Chinese restaurants or hamburger bars. Apart from anything else, sandwiches are not particularly photogenic.

Neon signs situated inside but visible from outside are definitely worth considering although they are expensive. Depending on how close they are to the front of the shop they might require local authority permission.

Exterior blackboards are also useful to advertise the introduction of a new sandwich or salad – and it's a good idea to do this from time to time. Never stand still. They do get tatty-looking quite quickly and are affected by rain so make sure you keep them looking smart. Remember your image.

Once established, some people choose to have the exterior blackboards painted professionally with details of the main items on sale. It looks professional and it means you don't have to keep on re-chalking them. Again, art students will often be happy to undertake such work.

> **However, if you do this, or if you have things professionally signwritten on exterior walls, be sure the details are not going to change. Nothing looks worse than elegantly written opening hours which have been amateurishly altered by the boss (who has discovered that staying open until 7.00 pm is pointless).**

When advertising for staff or informing your customers of holiday closures you will no doubt want to put temporary signs in the window. Make them look as professional as possible. It sends a message to your prospective employees as well as the public at large.

You can produce good quality notices with your computer. What's more you can store them so that when the next vacancy occurs you just need to print off another copy, making any minor adjustments that might be necessary.

Spelling on signs

Quite a few of the words which will feature regularly on your menus and signs are easy to misspell. Do try to be accurate. It will strike a lot of people as amateurish if they see a sign which advertises the delights of 'Mozarela and corriander on toasted focacia with an expresso or a capucino'. Can you spot the spelling mistakes? There are seven.

The ability of computers to produce good signs is just one of the many things they can do to help the small business. I will talk more about them elsewhere in the book.

Interior signs:

◆ blackboards,
◆ backlit plastic signs (possibly incorporating photographs of the products available),
◆ laminated notices or menus,
◆ plastic boards, usually black, full of holes, (like a Chinese chequers board) into which you insert white plastic letters and figures to give details of your products and prices,
◆ whiteboards on which you can write with a marker pen,
◆ hanging signs,
◆ posters advertising the products of a particular company.

Internal signs are more about providing information to the customer once inside the shop. What is most important is that they be clear, legible and readily understood.

> **Legal disclaimer:** In this litigious day and age it is probably a good idea to put up a sign pointing out that you are unable to guarantee that the products you sell are free from nuts or nut products. The fact is you don't know exactly what has gone into every single thing you sell. This is necessary because a very few people have extreme allergic reactions to nuts, which can be fatal.
>
> Of course, if you sell a product such as walnut bread it should always be clearly labelled. Avoid the indiscriminate use of nuts as a garnish.

As with exterior signs, the possibilities are endless. You must consider them all and choose signs which fit in with your particular vision. A few thoughts:

◆ One of the real bores about signs comes when you need to put the prices up. You spent hours painstakingly writing out your list of sandwiches on the blackboard. All you need to do is change the prices. Should you do the whole lot again or just wipe out the prices and put in the new ones as neatly as possible? The answer is probably the former but the reality is more likely to be the latter.

◆ If you are changing blackboards, it is best to wipe off the writing and then paint the blackboard with blackboard paint available from DIY stores. It's a bit more work but it doesn't take long and it looks so much smarter.

◆ It is possible to have blackboards professionally and permanently painted. Sometimes this involves some artwork round the edges, sometimes artwork plus your list of sandwiches. In the latter case make sure the prices are not permanently marked. Problems can arise if you stop doing a particular sandwich – blanking out can look very messy.

◆ The plastic boards with holes for letters of course allow for changing the prices – but to be honest they're pretty downmarket-looking.

◆ Whiteboards don't look great either, but one small one to give information on things that change daily, such as the kind of soup on offer, is probably OK.

◆ It may seem like stating the obvious, but if you install hanging signs make sure they are very secure and that customers will not bump their heads against them.

One final word of warning: it's easy to see signs as less important in the great scheme of things, to concentrate your energies on the quality of the food and worry about the expensive fridge you've ordered. These things are important of course but for customers the signs are vital. They should allow them quickly and easily to see what's on offer and how much it will cost. In addition, the more tastefully and professionally the signs are done the better the image of the shop.

> Don't do what we did with our first shop. As we got closer to opening we had lots to do but we kept putting off thinking about the main sign advertising the sandwiches plus prices. In the end I was up a ladder the night before we opened writing out our list on a large whiteboard with a marker pen. I look back on it now and cringe. I was dog tired and it looked dreadful. I wonder how we got any business at all. We ended up getting large professionally constructed blackboards which looked great – but this was weeks after we had opened and it caused much inconvenience.

Staff image

In Chapter Eight I shall deal with various issues relating to staff: hiring and firing, conditions of employment and so on. Here I shall say something about staff image, which is or should be part of your vision for your shop.

> **There really is no point in selling the most delectable sandwiches in Britain if the people working behind the counter are sullen, unwelcoming, malodorous or dressed in torn or dirty clothes**

One of the things you will learn about running a business is that you must have rules and standards *which must be enforced*. This is particularly true when dealing with staff. If you don't enforce rules then the staff will dictate many aspects of how your business is run. Given your responsibilities to customers and obligations under the law in respect of health and safety and so on, this could lead to serious problems.

Staff in sandwich-coffee bars tend to leave on a fairly regular basis, meaning that, in the absence of clear and firm guidance from the top, customers could experience lack of consistency. It's your job to ensure that so far as possible the quality of service delivered is reliable and predictable.

So far as image and staff are concerned I think the main points to consider are these:

1. Attitude and manners. It is vital that the people who work for you display reasonable enthusiasm for the job. It is also important that they do not suddenly become moody or withdrawn for no apparent reason. There is no room to hide in a sandwich bar and such behaviour affects the whole atmosphere in the shop; it's unfair on the other staff and unpleasant for customers. We all have problems at home from time to time but unless it's something really serious, staff (and you) must learn to get over it and concentrate on the job in hand.

2. Staff must have a smart and clean appearance. It would be impossible to make specific comments about what is and is not acceptable. That is a matter for you and depends on the image you wish to project. For some, five-day stubble and rings through noses might be absolutely fine. For others they would be out of the question – staff would be expected to be clean shaven or to wear smart white blouses. *The point is that cleanliness and some* *kind of dress code are essential.* From a health and hygiene point of view staff should not wear lots of make up or strong deoderants which could be transferred to food. Long hair should always be tied back.

3. Uniform? At one end of the spectrum you have places where the staff can wear what they like. The trouble is that even if they are well turned-out the impression given can be amateurish: a random group of people just like the customers who happen to be on the other side of the serve-over.

At the other end of the spectrum you get a lot of places now where staff must wear a uniform designed to allow no room for individuality. This is particularly true of the large fast food chains.

It seems to me that neither end of the spectrum is right for a small independent sandwich-coffee bar. I think the minimum 'uniform' should be an apron with the name of your sandwich bar on it and or your logo. An apron is a practical, hygienic necessity – it protects clothes and provides a pocket to keep all sorts of things in. In addition it makes a clear distinction between staff and customers. The presence of your name or logo reinforces the corporate image. The other obvious possibility is some kind of headwear. Hats have the added advantage of helping to cover and secure longer hair.

> **You have to strike a balance between what fits in with your vision, what is practical and desirable from a business point of view and what is affordable.**

Choosing packaging

If the food's good enough you could say that the packaging shouldn't matter. Perhaps. However, whether it's underwear from the supermarket or take-away hamburgers, people are used to and expect quite a sophisticated level of packaging nowadays.

By 'packaging' I am talking about:

◆ film-fronted paper bags for sandwiches which must be the right size for the range of sandwiches you will sell. You will probably need at least two sizes.
◆ clear plastic boxes for a variety of salads (or indeed for certain sizes of sandwiches, especially those made with baguettes). These sometimes come with a 'spork' (a cross between a spoon and a fork) attached.

- sticky labels for sealing the bags.
- carrier bags (plastic or, better in my view, paper),
- cup carriers – made out of egg box type paper; they enable you to transport more than one container of hot liquid at the same time. They also make it easier to transport hot drinks in cars.
- plastic polystyrene or paper cups for drinks and soup. The plastic ones can be clear – suitable for cold drinks such as smoothies and freshly squeezed orange juice.
(Sticky labels, carrier bags and some cups can all have your logo and a bit of advertising blurb on the side).

ONE TIP ON THE SUBJECT OF DRINKS CONTAINERS: for hot drinks always use containers with sip lids. They allow people to drink their coffee or tea without having to remove the lid – *it's more user-friendly and helps to keep the drinks hotter longer.*

There are new packaging products coming onto the market all the time, so it's a good idea to subscribe to the trade magazine *International Sandwich and Snack News* in order to keep abreast of such innovations.

What are the advantages of good quality packaging?

Good quality packaging is practical, it looks professional and it can advertise your business.

- You've gone to the trouble of lovingly preparing a half baguette containing avocado, prawns and herb salad. The last thing you want is to have any problems putting your little work of art in its bag, with bits falling out all over the place. The customer will not be impressed and you will waste time. Such problems are avoided and your confidence increased by having the right size and quality of bag or other container – especially when it is firmly sealed with a sticky label.
- Whilst the quality of the food is paramount, customers will be impressed and reassured by the professional appearance which good quality packaging creates.
- Don't underestimate the power of packaging to advertise you and your product. If somebody is sitting in the sun contentedly eating a sandwich from its bag, passers-by may well notice the logo on the sticky label. Similarly, carrier bags can display your name in quite a concentrated area around your shop. Remember, people don't tend to travel far to buy their sandwiches.
- One slight problem with this is the customer who drops litter in the street. I have

noticed this on occasion near our shop. There is a risk of guilt by association and I invariably pick it up.

Points to remember about packaging:

◆ Always include a unit cost for packaging when arriving at new prices for your sandwiches.
◆ Don't be too ambitious with colours. It's usually sufficient to use one colour for your logo and any associated writing. This will make a strong enough impression, and using more than one colour makes the job considerably more expensive.

Producing printed menus

You're going to have prominent signs inside the shop giving full details of the sandwiches on offer, so why do you need printed menus as well?

◆ Particularly before and just after opening, handing out menus is a particularly good way of creating awareness of, and interest in, your new venture amongst local shops and businesses.
◆ By making them easily available to customers in the shop you're giving out information and also advertising your products. They might take them away and tell their friends.
◆ Assuming you will be doing some administrative work from home then printed menus will be extremely useful at various times:

    a When reviewing the list of sandwiches and considering new ones to include and poor sellers to discontinue.

    b When considering price increases.

    c When updating the general layout or design of the menu itself or when looking for inspiration for new ideas.

◆ If you intend to do outside catering (see Chapter Eleven for more on this subject) then I think it is a good idea to work out separate menus for the purpose. Organisations interested in an outside catering service will not be too impressed if they have to send someone round to the shop to take details from a blackboard – or if they need to have a lengthy menu explained to them over the phone. They want to be able to look at their options in the comfort of their offices before making a choice which they can phone in at their leisure.

You could pay professional printers to produce your menus – but you can produce perfectly high quality, professional looking menus on your own computer. They can be stored on your PC and e-mailed to customers or amended with ease when you increase prices.

Selecting a colour scheme

There can be a tendency to regard choice of colours as a minor matter to be dealt with 'nearer the time', but this is a bad idea. Once you start having to make decisions about the matters talked about in this chapter – aprons, labels, interior and exterior signs, paintwork and so on – you have to be aware of colour. They don't all have to be done in the same colour but they do have to go together and in my view it's a good idea to have one dominant colour.

Some points to consider:
◆ there can be a tendency for new businesses (a bit like new parents choosing a name for a child), to think that if they choose a colour which is dramatically different and striking somehow their business will be too. But the bottom line is that the quality of the food is paramount. Stick to non-controversial colours.

> **Your colour scheme will be an integral element of your image and merits a good deal of thought.**

◆ Drive round your town or city and look at as many shops as possible for ideas. See which colours look good – and which don't.
◆ As a general rule you should have stronger shades on the exterior of your shop; it helps to make you stand out and there will not be so many colours competing with each other. Strong shades inside tend to dominate and 'reduce' the internal space and make it more difficult for pictures or photographs to stand out. Inside you don't want the colours on the walls and ceiling to attract attention to themselves.
◆ I don't recommend white for inside or outside. It's rather stark and unsubtle. It also gets dirty quickly. Very dark colours also show up the dirt and are, in any event, generally unsuitable for the interior.
◆ You should repaint inside and out at least once every three years. As time goes by there is inevitably a gradual deterioration in the paintwork. You don't notice it so much because you're in the place every day – however, the customers will.

REMEMBER: when repainting try to choose a time when the shop is closed – summer or Christmas holidays perhaps – you really shouldn't be serving food in the midst of paint and turpentine aromas!

CHAPTER FIVE

Bread and Butter Issues:
Food and Drink, Staff and You

We now come to some of the most important issues to consider when setting up a new sandwich-coffee bar: the actual products you and your staff will sell to the public. This is what it's all about. And things have moved on rather a lot since the Earl of Sandwich put some cheese between a couple of slices of bread so that he could stay at the gaming table without having to waste time going for lunch.

It's easy to get carried away by the interesting – even glamourous – aspects of giving your new business a sexy image. These are important and people will see part of the 'brand value' of your place as being the general feelgood factor of the surroundings and the ambience of the place. However, you will only build up a strong customer base if the products you sell are of a consistently good standard and priced at a level people regard as giving them value for money.

> **By the time you open you must have a tried and tested range of core sandwiches and other products which you and your staff can prepare with confidence. Customers will not be impressed if you appear unsure about what you're doing. First impressions count for a lot. You will need to work out well in advance a range of issues related to the kinds of sandwiches and other food products you are going to sell.**

Creating your sandwich list

In Chapter One I talked about the kind of initial research you should carry out. Part of this involved visiting and trying out as many comparable businesses as possible. While doing this, try to get hold of lots of menus or sandwich lists to pore over at home. You should then gradually compile your initial list from the following:

◆ particular sandwiches that during your research you found especially appealing
◆ other people's menus or lists
◆ the internet – quite a lot of sandwich bars have web sites, including a lot in America

◆ your own ideas – however off the wall at this stage

◆ ideas taken from magazines, including the trade magazine *International Sandwich and Snack News* which regularly publishes recipes dreamt up by finalists in best sandwich competitions

◆ recipe books – you will see a few specific sandwich ideas in general recipe books plus *countless other concoctions not intended as sandwich ingredients which might just give you the basis for an unusual sandwich.* A lot of people nowadays are looking for new ideas to stimulate their jaded palates and this kind of lateral thinking could give you a competitive edge.

> Before we opened our first shop I looked through numerous general recipe books. One recipe I came across that particularly appealed to me was for aubergine caviare. It's a kind of vegetarian pâté. I liked the idea of something with aubergines (which we hadn't thought of) and I was taken by the unusual name. It was slow to catch on at first but when it did it soon became an established favourite with some of our regular customers. It still is.

New ideas and old favourites

Clearly you have to be aware of people's tastes in your neighbourhood; but wherever that may be, *it's important to strike a balance between well-known favourites (however dull they may seem) and more exotic creations.*

If you don't have cheese, egg mayonnaise and tuna mayonnaise on your menu you will undoubtedly lose customers. You could, of course, introduce some variety by having one plain tuna mayonnaise and another with red and orange peppers or red onions added to the mix.

You should also ensure that you have some more interesting and unusual items on offer. I've come across emu and ostrich sandwiches; really the possibilities are unlimited. It's all about offering a large and interesting choice. Your business will probably rely heavily on regulars and your selection should allow them to be a bit daring now and then.

> **Introducing an occasional new sandwich can be a great way of creating interest. You can include a 'newsflash' type section on your street sandwich board and put a few notices up inside the shop. Keep one good one back to introduce six weeks after you open. This way you can create renewed publicity after the initial interest has waned. Also, always be on the look-out for new ideas – especially those suggested by customers. We have introduced a number of new sandwiches in this way over the years.**

Festivals and seasonal changes can provide reasons for advertising the introduction of new ideas. For instance, every December we do a Christmas sandwich with turkey and stuffing. It always sells well.

Introducing new ideas in this way doesn't necessarily increase the number of customers you have. The main thing is that it will help to maintain the interest and loyalty of the ones you've already got.

Responding to unexpected events

Not long after we opened our first shop, the BSE crisis hit the headlines. We suddenly found that the demand for certain meat sandwiches, especially beef and horseradish, plummeted. We could simply have stopped selling the ones which ceased to be popular and waited for demand to recover. However, this would have significantly reduced our selection. As soon as I realised the scale of the problem I spoke to our butcher. He pointed out that the problem with beef had arisen because of the kind of feed the animals had been given. He also pointed out that deer simply grazed in fields and that BSE should not be an issue in their case. Within days we were selling venison accompanied by either mint jelly or cranberry sauce. Although not big sellers they are still on our menu.

In those difficult days one place even resorted to selling alligator sandwiches! I never did find out who their supplier was. I do hope it wasn't Edinburgh Zoo.

Made to order or made in advance?

By this stage you should have observed a considerable number of sandwich-coffee bars in action. You should therefore be forming a view about whether your sandwiches will be made to order or made in advance.

I suggest you also put yourself in the place of the customer and ask yourself the question: which would I prefer?

Made to order means exactly what it says. You don't start making the sandwich until the customer has explained what they want. A lot of customers prefer this. Not only can they get exactly what they want, they can watch the sandwich being made before their very eyes and satisfy themselves that it's all being done properly.

> **You will find a degree of suspicion on the part of some people. It is not uncommon for a customer to ask for a sandwich to be made up even though there is one of exactly the kind he wants on the shelf which was made an hour previously. When you try to reassure them they suspect it was actually made last week, is horribly stale and that you're just trying to save money.**

Advantages of made to order

◆ **Flexibility and choice for the customer.** You can offer unlimited permutations.

◆ **Less waste.** If you have a quieter day then you don't use up lots of ingredients making up sandwiches for the shelf which nobody buys. You just get left with a pile of bread – much less costly.

◆ **You save time in the first part of the day.** You don't have to make up lots of sandwiches for the shelves.

◆ **Your internal signs can be shorter.** They simply need to give an indication of the breads and main ingredients available and a formula for working out prices depending on the combination chosen. You probably won't need to change them very often.

◆ **Quite a lot of customers prefer it** and are prepared to put up with a wait.

> **Just imagine the way you would make a sandwich at home with all your personal likes and dislikes. Don't you think it would be attractive to a lot of people to have this service available?**

Disadvantages of made to order

1. **The time factor.** You might save time in the morning but you will find that serving customers at the busy times takes considerably longer – especially if you have someone who needs time to agonise over every single option. And you really can't avoid this. Customers must be offered a choice of everything from type of bread to butter, margarine or nothing. If you go for this choice your staff must be trained to go through a checklist. *It can be tedious but it's all part of the service.*

2. **Extra staff costs.** As a result of the extra time involved you may need to have more staff on at lunchtime.

3. **Lack of flexibility.** If you have a very busy day, even if you have extra help at lunchtime, you can't really speed things up and customers don't have the option of grabbing a ready-made sandwich off the shelf.

4. Quite a lot of customers are in a hurry at lunchtime. They're not bothered about having things made up for them. They don't want to hang around for long and may be deterred by lengthy queues.

5. A lot more mental arithmetic. If somebody buys a sandwich off the shelf it is already priced. If their sandwich is made to order you have to work out what it all costs: type of bread, ingredients, plus extras.

Your decision

So what's best? You must make your own decisions, but in my view the best course for a small independent operation is to have a mixture of the two options – *and thus offer your valued customers the best of both worlds.* Unfortunately you will also take on some disadvantages – but it is part of your challenge to manage and mitigate them.

You will need to :

- Become an expert on isobars, high pressure and weather fronts. Most sandwich-coffee bars are affected by the weather. *If you know the weather will be bad, make up less for the shelves and order less bread. This way you will have less unwanted sandwiches at the end of the day and save money.*
- Become familiar with the patterns of your customers – for example, student holidays, busy tourist times, whatever factors are likely to affect your business – and make up sandwiches and order bread accordingly. In addition, keep notes of unusual trading conditions so that you are ready for them in the following year.

> Take one example from my own experience: Saturdays are usually 30% to 40% quieter than weekdays. However, during our first year we were completely overwhelmed on one particular Saturday. Unbeknown to us there was a local festival near our shop which attracted thousands of people – and which had not been well advertised. We were completely unprepared. We were queued out all day and kept on having to go out and buy more bread from wherever we could get it. Good business you may say, but I'm sure to the customers it all looked really amateurish – and for the staff it was hell. We made a note of this in our financial record of the day – a good place to note these things because one way or another you have to look at your books quite often – and we were not caught out again the following year.

I think it's also a good idea to keep a note of extreme weather conditions. Figures from the previous year which might appear surprisingly poor can sometimes be explained by the fact that there was unseasonably bad weather at the time.

It will take a full year's trading to gain an insight into the general pattern.

◆ If a queue builds up because sandwiches are being made to order, train your staff to fast-track people who just want to pay for a sandwich they have picked up off the shelf. It might well be a good idea to operate two tills at busy times or one express till for those who don't want a sandwich made up. So long as this is all done in a transparent and sensible way other customers will not see it as queue-jumping but rather sensible management – they too might just want a quick sandwich on occasion and will like the idea that they won't have to wait for ages, even when the shop is busy.

◆ Be well organised in the early part of the day. Have a list of sandwiches to be made up for the shelf (variable in light of weather conditions, etc.) which should be ready by a certain time. It is vital that you have finished preparing these sandwiches before the customers start arriving in numbers. *If you do this you will be properly prepared for the lunchtime rush and will be better able to meet the needs of all customers.*

◆ Consider the possibility of customers faxing or e-mailing their orders in during the morning. You can then make the orders up and have them ready and waiting at lunchtime. If you do this, have a deadline when orders must be in by – probably 11.00 am. *Don't encourage orders by phone.* This takes up a lot of valuable time and there is too much scope for errors. Harness technology to work for you by easing the pressure at busy times.

Two final points about sandwiches made up for the shelf:

1. You'll save a lot of time and effort if, rather than labelling each sandwich individually, you allocate spaces on your refrigerated display shelves for piles of particular sandwiches. All you need to do is insert labels in the plastic pockets running along the front edge of the shelves with the name of the sandwich.

2. Aim for the average taste. If a customer wants to have a sandwich made to order with enough mustard to inflict third degree burns on the roof of his mouth that's his privilege. Sandwiches on the shelf must be made such as to appeal to and not offend a wide variety of tastes. I think it's probably best not to put on salt or pepper at all – have free sachets available near the till.

Buying in pre-prepared sandwiches

You can, of course, save yourself a huge amount of work and reduce your wage bill by buying in mass-produced stuff from one of the big sandwich manufacturing factories. This would mean that you would be selling the same kind of sandwiches as you see in motorway service stations and some supermarkets. This may be appropriate if you want to be freed up to concentrate on the coffee/tea/juice and cakes side of things or if, for instance, you want to have an internet café. However, if you are serious about delivering quality sandwiches with individual character, buying in sandwiches is not an option.

A word about mayonnaise

Mayonnaise is used widely in sandwiches. It tastes good, is great for binding things together and, to be honest, can help to pad the sandwich out a bit. However, not everyone likes mayonnaise. If you make sandwiches up to order this is not a problem, but if you don't I suggest you always have a few sandwiches on the shelf which don't contain mayonnaise.

Other food and drinks

To say that sandwich-coffee bars only sell sandwiches and coffee would be a bit like saying fish and chip shops only sell fish and chips. It might have been true once but it certainly isn't now. In general, even the small independent has to be prepared to sell a variety of, for want of a better expression, food products.

The customer base is bigger, but customers have a larger and more varied spectrum of outlets to choose from. Although you will always hope to have a good base of regulars, many people don't have any strong allegiance. I suppose you could call them floating voters. It's your job to hook as many of them as you can by having an appealing and varied selection on offer.

However, don't forget: there is no point in introducing lots of new ideas if you cannot deliver consistently good quality in all areas.

Are you starting to feel overwhelmed and dismayed at the idea of having to become a purveyor of lots of things beyond the simple sandwich? Well the good news is that it's not nearly as complicated as you might think. *In fact, it's surprisingly easy to give the impression of selling lots of interesting things without having to make a lot of changes from the basic concept.*

> Shortly after we opened our second shop, an outlet selling tortilla wraps opened about a hundred yards away from us amidst a fanfare of publicity. Wraps had become rather trendy and we were a bit concerned at this development – especially since students make up a large proportion of our customer base and tend to like fashionable new ideas. I decided we had to start selling wraps. All that was actually involved was finding a supplier for wraps (cash and carry), putting a sign up inside the shop detailing our range of wraps together with their prices, ordering some clear plastic boxes from our suppliers, having a mini awareness-raising campaign (good publicity for us) and that was it.
>
> The key was the serve-over (or delicatessen unit). This was stocked with our range of sandwich ingredients and all we needed to do was put them in wraps instead of sandwiches.

When introducing something new like this it's a good idea to think of some new combinations and of course you can make them up to order as well. The quantities you serve in sandwiches should be roughly the same for wraps (or indeed salads) so that the prices should be comparable.

Toasted sandwiches

Similarly, you can offer a range of toasted sandwiches. For this you will need a contact grill (which you will sometimes hear referred to as a Panini grill) – i.e. one which has two halves, both heated, with the sandwich being pressed between them for a few minutes. Cheese is particularly popular in toasted sandwiches because it melts. In fact, some places refer to toasted sandwiches as 'melts'.

Pre-cooked meals

Another possibility is pre-cooked meals, e.g. chilli con carne or vegetable lasagne. There are plenty of suppliers of such convenience meals which usually come in sealed plastic containers. One basic microwave should be well up to heating them. The disadvantages are that they sometimes take quite a long time to cook (up to ten minutes) and they don't always cook evenly.

Soups

Soup is popular in all but the warmest months. You can now buy in quite interesting soups from specialist suppliers which are really not bad. I'm not talking about well-known brands of tinned soups. However, if you are going to use a home kitchen then home-made will be best – cheaper and tastier. Just use recipes featuring whatever vegetables are in season at a particular time and this will keep the cost down. To keep things simple use vegetable stock. Vegetarians wouldn't accept anything else and carnivores won't mind. (I shall discuss issues relating to preparing food at home in Chapters Six and Nine.)

Salads

Salads can be served in clear plastic boxes and based around sandwich ingredients displayed on a bed of lettuce – possibly just made to order. They are popular in these weight-conscious times.

Ice-creams and ice lollies

Some of the large suppliers will sell you freezers at favourable prices in the hope that you will sell their products. Not surprisingly such freezers come with advertisements for their products, but you are free to stock whatever you like. And in a further effort to get you into the habit of buying from them they will probably give you a stock voucher for an amount similar to the cost of the freezer – so you could say it doesn't really cost you anything at all. You should check with the ice-cream companies to see what deals are on the go at any particular time.

Don't have too many varieties. Pick a reasonable cross section of the bigger names. For something a little bit different you can also get individual tubs of sorbets.

Scoop ice cream sold in cones and wafers is very appealing, but you must be very careful to maintain correct temperatures in accordance with the manufacturer's instructions. Bear in mind that the season in Britain is fairly short, the unit takes up a fair bit of space and is not cheap to buy. It's important to capitalise on this by means of street or very obvious window advertising.

Ethnic foods

Foods which might appeal to particular ethnic or other groups in your area can be successful. Where we are located items such as pakoras and samosas are particularly popular. They can be heated in a microwave.

Vegetarian/vegan foods

You could offer special lines which would appeal to vegans, i.e., which contain no animal produce whatever (no dairy products, eggs, etc.). It would be quite straightforward to allot an area of the refrigerated display unit to such items. As a general rule, for the ease of customers, it is a good idea to have your pre-prepared sandwiches in clearly identified sections: meat, fish, vegetarian (and possibly vegan).

The healthy angle

Have particular sandwiches and low calorie, sweet-tasting things specifically aimed at those trying to lose weight and advertise the fact. You should also have sachets of sweetener available.

Cakes, patisserie, croissants and gateaux

All of these can be attractive additions to what you offer to the public. They look good and are generally popular. You will, however, need to have space (ideally refrigerated) set aside for them which is both visible to your customers and easily accessible by you. This should not be the main serve-over unit containing your meats and other sandwich ingredients. It might mean a new refrigerated unit – a considerable extra cost for a comparatively marginal item. In addition, there might be space problems in smaller units. Whatever, all such items should be kept under cover.

From the start we have sold home-made cakes and tray-bakes. I think good home-made items are best though there are now some specialist cake manufacturers whose standards are quite high.

The only thing to watch out for is that some items have a short shelf life. Since they can be quite expensive if bought in, there is the possibility of considerable waste if demand tails off – there are only so many you can take home.

Fresh fruit salads

These will keep for three or four days in a sealed plastic container in a refrigerated display unit. Avoid bananas. A tin or two of tropical fruit cocktail added to some more mundane fruits makes for a very pleasing and refreshing snack or sweet.

Iced teas and cold chocolate drinks

Obviously these will probably only sell in the summer. In addition there are frozen coffee drinks known as 'frappaccinos.'

Floats

These are cream sodas with a scoop of ice-cream floating on the top. You can have a variety of flavours by the addition of different syrups.

Salads made with pasta, rice or chopped potatoes

These would probably be made up in advance and displayed in your refrigerated unit. Salads like this (and fruit salads) might only be viable during the warmer months.

Sushi

Sushi is quite commonplace now. The difficulty here is that the unit cost to you is reasonably high, so if it doesn't sell you could lose a fair bit of money. Trial it for a couple of weeks and advertise heavily to see if it will take off where you are.

Fruit smoothies and milkshakes

You can buy fruit smoothies in plastic bottles from your cash and carry – but they're never as good as ones you have made fresh. Look in recipe books to give you ideas for flavours. Similarly with milkshakes, you can buy powder or syrup which you mix with milk, but real milk mixed with real ice-cream is best.

Individual pies or pizzas

Make sure they are good quality. Try them yourself and order a selection.

Fruit

And don't forget a selection of fresh fruit – increasingly popular in these health-conscious times. Don't have Golden Delicious apples – they're utterly tasteless. Granny Smith's are always popular, as are Braeburn and Cox's Pippins. Bananas are also very popular. Make sure old tired-looking fruit is removed. Do what they do in New York delis: polish the apples, especially the big red ones. It's those little touches....

Imagine the different signs needed to advertise the various ideas I have mentioned. You can see that it is not difficult to give the impression of a busy, buzzy shop overflowing with options – it's what the customer likes.

Dealing with leftover sandwiches

If every person who has ever sold sandwiches could have one wish I bet it would be this: to know in advance exactly how many sandwiches would be needed on a particular day. Sometimes it does all work out perfectly and you end up with no bread, no made up sandwiches and an empty soup kettle – no waste. However, this is the exception not the rule.

There are a number of approaches to this issue which are not mutually exclusive. Follow what works for you

1. Keep your bread order low and only have a limited quantity of soup available

In this way, unless you are very quiet indeed you will find that there is little if any waste at the end of the day. The trouble is on many days you will spend lots of time apologising:

You: Sorry, soup's finished.
Customer: But it's only half past twelve.
You: Yes I know, but last week I had to throw some soup out, terrible waste.

Do you think the customer will be sympathetic? Not in the slightest. If this sort of thing happens regularly customers will be irritated and may well be inclined to take their business elsewhere. The same will be true if you have to explain repeatedly that you have run out of focaccia or baguette or indeed particular sandwich ingredients. If you want to follow this approach then you really must try to judge it well – and the longer you're in business the better able you will be to do this.

However, you do run the risk of providing a limited service and appearing pennypinching – more interested in your needs than those of the customer.

2. Leave sandwiches on your refrigerated display shelves for two or three days

This approach certainly means you don't need to worry so much about misjudging the number of sandwiches you make up on a particular day. But it also means you will have to be aware of the freshness of the sandwiches on the shelf. You could end up with sandwiches of different ages being displayed simultaneously. If you were the customer, which one would you buy?

The practice of selling sandwiches which are up to two or even three days old is fairly widespread. People do seem to accept it. It is not something I have ever done. I just don't think sandwiches, the original fast food, were ever meant to be kept for more than a few hours. The quality diminishes – not least because the bread is liable to become soggy. If you planned to go for a picnic on Sunday afternoon, would you make up the sandwiches on Friday morning?

However, so long as you make up the sandwiches yourself for sale in your shop it is legal to display them in this way. Bear in mind, that if anybody does have cause for complaint you will have to be able to show that you had good reason to believe that the sandwiches would continue to be of an acceptable quality. This could be achieved by testing various kinds of sandwiches over a number of days to see what kinds of things can go wrong: increased sogginess, stale flavour, prawns going off and so on.

Whilst it is not essential, you would be well advised to have a 'durability indication' on any sandwich kept beyond the day it's made – i.e. a use- or sell-by date. You might even want to give some sandwiches to your local public analyst. If they found that your sandwiches were biologically acceptable after two days then you would obviously have a good defence against anyone complaining about such sandwiches.

3. Install a bake-off oven and make some or all of your own bread

Bake-off ovens have been a godsend, especially now that they are readily available, easy to use and need not involve substantial start-up costs. You can have bread from freezer to operating table in about 20 minutes. Bake-off ovens allow you to make it up as you go along, to respond to the level of business on a particular day. This is in stark contrast to the usual situation of having to make a decision the day before when placing your order. They are used most commonly for baguettes. They are simple to bake and in my experience the results are reliable and excellent. As you will see when you start to receive catalogues from the big catering suppliers, there are many other products which can be produced in them.

Despite this, if you want to offer a wide range of breads you will probably still have to buy some in from local bakers. Bake-off ovens are not really suitable for the humble roll. Most sandwich bars order in a fairly large quantity of rolls each day and it would not be practical to try to bake these plus baguettes and croissants in the morning.

Another plus point is that bake-off ovens create a delectable aroma which adds to the customer appeal of the shop.

A bake-off oven helps you to be in control; you don't have to order everything in the day before when you're not sure what demand will be like. It can also be used for pastries and savoury snacks which could enable you to expand your repertoire. An oven suitable for most medium sized sandwich bars simply requires a 13 amp plug, although larger more powerful ovens may need to be hard-wired.

ONE OTHER POINT ABOUT BAKE-OFFS

Since it is now possible to bake reasonably large quantities of baguettes some places have a display in the front of the shop selling plain baguettes or croissants. I see the point: it looks good and it offers the customer more choice. But the trouble is that some people will buy a baguette and then go somewhere else to buy some avocados and tomato and put together a little picnic. You might sell a baguette for 70p and make 20p. A third-baguette with avocado, tomato and salad you might sell for about £2.60, allowing scope for making a lot more than 20p. Let delicatessens and bakers' shops sell bread on its own – you should sell sandwiches.

International Sandwich and Snack News will provide details of suppliers of bake-off ovens. You can also get information from the big catering suppliers which supply many of the products (not just baguettes) which can be cooked in the ovens. Alternatively just do a Google search.

4. Have plentiful supplies and be positive about what to do with what's left

The customer generally likes to be presented with a good choice. Indeed marketing people will tell you that the sight of large stocks of particular items will make people more likely to buy. I'm sure also that the converse is true – people do tend to be unimpressed by the sight of one or two sandwiches dotted about the shelves, those not chosen during the lunchtime rush.

As I said at the start of the book, some level of waste is inevitable when dealing with perishables. Here are a few thoughts on how to make a virtue out of a necessity:

◆ If you have children, take the made-up sandwiches home, put them in the fridge and use them for packed lunches the next day. You will probably find that some of them won't last that long because children do tend to like the immediacy of sandwiches. (Be warned: this can cause annoyance when it spoils their appetite for the evening meal!)

◆ If you have a particularly quiet day and it's obvious there will be a lot of sandwiches left, phone a friend or two and invite them round for an impromptu sandwich supper. With the money you save on your evening meal why not buy in some good beer or wine to go with the meal?

◆ Bread can be frozen. It keeps pretty well for a month or so. You can simply take it out of the freezer and allow it to defrost. A quicker way is to put it in a microwave, select auto defrost and blast it for 20 seconds or so. Either way, the flavour is improved if you heat the bread briefly in the oven or under the grill. (In the case of auto-defrosted bread this should be done after the microwaving).

◆ Come to an arrangement with a local charity for homeless people whereby they arrange to collect bread and/or sandwiches that are left over at the end of the day. Make sure this is done through proper channels because with the best will in the world you do not want a lot of homeless people appearing in the shop looking for hand-outs.

◆ Use bread left over as an excuse to go for a walk in a park where you can feed the birds – seriously, it's a very pleasant way of spending an hour or two. My favourite thing is getting the seagulls to catch rolled up bits of bread in mid air!

◆ Be philosophical and accept the inevitability of waste; throw it out and aim to have less waste tomorrow. It is all tax deductible after all.

Clearly you will take some food home on occasion. You may also buy the odd thing at the cash and carry for the house. Bear in mind that the HMRC expect this and that your accountant may well ask you for a notional figure for the amount of food bought for the business which is eaten at home.

Offering a range of cold drinks

Balance a good selection of cold drinks with sensible economics.

Put yourself into the shoes of an imaginary customer and consider what kind of choice you would like to be presented with. There are hundreds if not thousands of drinks available. However, many are just variations on a theme so a balanced selection of perhaps 25 or 30 drinks should have something for everyone.

◆ You should certainly have the most famous brand names – and don't forget to have 'diet' equivalents.

◆ You should have some juices which are entirely free of sugar.

◆ As with the sandwiches I think it's a good idea to include a few of the more exotic things.

◆ Whatever the health-conscious may think of them, energy drinks are very popular just now, especially with teenagers and students.

- Flavoured milks (for some reason only ever available in chocolate, banana or strawberry flavours) are steady sellers.
- Have some plain bottled water (fizzy and still) on sale.
- Keep up to date with new fashions (and fads) and be prepared to introduce new lines.
- Bottles with screw tops and sports tops are increasingly popular.
- Customers searching about for things can create chaos amongst the bottles and cans. It's annoying but you really must tidy them regularly to maintain your professional image.
- When restocking the drinks cabinet always make sure you or your staff bring the older bottles to the front. I know it's obvious and sensible but it doesn't always get done, which means that every now and then you find you've got a batch of cans which are past their sell-by date. It can also mean customers pick up a can which is not chilled, which is bad for business.

> You might notice that some of the bigger chains of sandwich-coffee bars now choose to have a very stripped down drinks selection; perhaps one famous best seller – you know the one – plus their own brands of fruit drinks and vegetable drinks, a mineral water and that's it. I think when starting up, you would be taking quite a risk in having such a limited choice.

Issues to consider if your life partner is also your business partner

1. What should you do if you and/or your partner are currently in paid employment?

Clearly one of you will have to give up work, but when? In my view the answer is as late in the day as humanly possible. You might be getting into the sandwich-coffee bar business because you are keen to get out of an unsatisfactory work situation, but the benefits of regular incomes for as long as possible should not be underestimated.

This is especially true since the first few months of trading are unlikely to be profitable. The numerous start-up costs will see to that. Frankly, you will be doing well to break even in the early stages.

2. Working patterns once your new business is established

It is, of course, quite possible for you and your partner to give up jobs and work full-time in the sandwich bar. The benefits are that you reduce your staff costs and you have greater confidence that things are being done properly. However, there are some points to bear in mind:

◆ Might it not be better to have the security of at least one steady income especially in the early stages?

◆ If one of you does keep a job going, full-time or part-time, this does not preclude that person from making a valuable contribution to the business. Someone's got to go to the cash and carry, deliver orders, do the banking, book-keeping and so on. These tasks can be fitted round a job. In fact, you will find that running a small business involves a lot of tasks like this which it would be awkward to get an employee to do.

◆ Do you necessarily want to spend your whole working day with your partner? Absence makes the heart grow fonder and all that – it also gives you more things to talk about over dinner.

◆ Be flexible in considering working patterns. You can do this. You're the boss, it's up to you. Perhaps you and your partner could each work part-time.

If you don't have a partner then perhaps you should consider working part-time leaving some time free during the day to attend the many other things that need to be done.

You should certainly be in the shop on a daily basis to keep your finger on the pulse and to ensure that your vision is being delivered to the public.

Your staffing needs

Assuming you are not going to try to do everything yourself or with your partner, you will need to hire staff. This is actually a task which can be left until much nearer the opening date and I will deal with it and other issues relating to staff later in the book. At this stage, however, there are some points to consider as you draw up your blueprint.

How many staff will you need?

How many full-time and part-time staff will you need? It's obviously important that you have the right amount of cover when you open. The difficulty is that you don't know how busy you will be – perhaps not very, initially. You may have staff who are under-employed. This is something you have to put up with for a while. You must think in terms of how you hope it will be a few weeks down the line and be staffed accordingly.

> **If it becomes obvious that you have one person too many then you should be prepared to shed them. Once you have made a decision you must act quickly. For someone who has not been in business before this can be one of the most difficult areas; but you have to face it because if you don't the problem will undoubtedly get worse.**

◆ Part-timers used to be cheaper to employ than full-timers. Now though, when it comes to the legal rights and entitlements of employees, there is no distinction between part-time and full-time. In my experience it is also uncommon to pay lower hourly rates to part-timers nowadays. There is one particular advantage in having a few part-timers. If they are able to be flexible then you can develop a small team on which you can draw if people go off sick. If you rely on one really good full-timer then if they are taken ill you have a problem.

Allocating tasks

Let's say you plan to have a good-sized sitting area in addition to the core sandwich-making operation – say ten tables. This means that a considerable amount of time will be spent taking orders, serving people and clearing tables. Do you think you should hire one person whose only job is to attend to these tasks? And what about behind the scenes? One person to take care of washing up, slicing cucumbers and tomatoes, crushing cardboard boxes for the rubbish and sweeping the floor? And you'll need someone – two people at least – to serve the customers, make sandwiches up to order, operate the till and deal with enquiries about deliveries and outside catering. What happens when one area of the operation is a bit quieter – can you then ask the person who does the washing up to serve tables? It all gets a bit complicated.

The answer is really quite simple. *It depends on the size of the operation.* If you plan to take on a large unit, possibly on different floors, then demarcation is not only desirable, it's essential for the smooth running of the place. However, for the great majority of small independent sandwich-coffee bars operating out of moderately sized units, it's vital that everybody does everything – *and that this is made clear to people at the interview stage.* There are always some jobs which are less popular than others, but working in a sandwich-coffee bar means taking the rough with the smooth. It's essential for efficiency that everybody understands this from the start and that staff don't feel they can turn their noses up at particular jobs. What's more, if you plan to work in the place yourself (as opposed to employing a manager) it's important that you set an example by taking your turn to do all the jobs involved in running the operation. It's a case of leading by example.

Opening hours

When planning your venture you will develop an idea of your preferred opening hours. But the fact is that you won't know what hours will work best for you until you have been trading for some time – I would say six months or so.

> **Whatever hours you decide upon at the start, be prepared to change them in the light of your trading experience. Don't pay for signs or sign writing which include specific opening hours; unless you're going to re-do the signs completely (immense waste of money), changes will inevitably look amateurish.**

Be prepared to experiment. You'll be surprised how even a minor change, opening quarter of an hour earlier, for instance, can ease your situation. It might mean that the journey to work is made easier because you miss the worst of the traffic.

You will almost certainly find that Saturdays and Sundays will be different from the rest of the week. If your trade is predominantly office people then it may not be worth opening at the weekend at all. If, however, you are in a tourist area then Saturday and Sunday could be your best days, although it might not be worth opening all year round. Experiment, yes, but don't flog a dead horse.

> Our first shop was located in George IV Bridge quite close to Edinburgh Castle Esplanade where each year they hold the Military Tattoo. We were aware that every evening for the four weeks of the Tattoo lots of buses full of tourists parked in George IV Bridge. So instead of closing at 5 o'clock we stayed open until 10pm. We stocked the shelves and waited for the deluge. Sure enough, regular as clockwork the buses arrived and disgorged masses of camera-toting tourists. Unfortunately the tourists had all eaten. They were marshalled with military precision by their guides and after five minutes of organised mayhem the place went dead. We got the occasional bus driver and the odd rebellious tourist. I remember one evening in particular when the best sale we had was when somebody bought four bags of crisps. That particular experiment lasted about a week!

Disabled customers

Whilst disabled people will only make up a small percentage of your customers it is neither difficult nor expensive to make your shop a bit more user-friendly for them.

◆ For people with impaired vision, produce a few copies of your menu in large print. This can be done easily on a PC.

◆ For blind people, produce a copy of the menu in braille. For assistance on this matter you should contact the Royal National Institute for the Blind (transcription service). Their number will be in your telephone directory. For an A4 sheet of 400 words the cost of producing a master will be in the region of £10 with copies costing about 50p each.

◆ For people with mobility problems (whether in wheelchairs or not), organise the furniture in the shop in such a way that there is an easy route in and out. Make sure that wheelchairs can cross the threshold of the shop easily. If the pavement is a few inches lower than the entrance a sloped piece of wood will easily do the trick.

◆ For deaf people, have a notepad and pencil readily available as they might find it easier to give their order in writing.

CHAPTER SIX

Suppliers

It would be a wonderful world indeed if you could obtain all the things you needed from one supplier. The savings on time spent phoning in orders and making sense of masses of paperwork from many organisations would equate to an extra week's holiday for you every year. In addition you would only have to put up with the disruption of one delivery every day. You would also be spared the weekly trip to the cash and carry.

The reality is very different. You will probably be surprised at the number of suppliers you will need.

Just consider a hypothetical order from one customer:

You: What can I get for you?

Customer: Small carrot and coriander soup.

You: And a sandwich?

Customer: Yes please. Could I have parma ham with smoked cheese on ciabatta with tomato, lettuce and cucumber.

You: Butter or margarine?

Customer: Butter, please.

You: Salt, pepper?

Customer: Pepper but no salt.

You: A little mayonnaise or creme fraiche?

Customer: Er, a little crème fraiche please. Oh and could I have some prawns and capers as well?

You (taking care not to show surprise or horror at the customer's choice – they sometimes give you viable new ideas): Certainly. Anything else?

Customer: Small cappuccino. Oh and I'll take something for the afternoon break as well; Milky Way, a piece of carrot cake, a carton of orange juice and a half litre of milk. Oh and it's such a warm day I think I'll treat myself to an ice cream as well.

You: I'll put it all in a bag for you – and here's a couple of napkins as well.

Nice order! How many suppliers would it need? The answer could be anything up to a dozen or so.

> **Incidentally, this somewhat eccentric sandwich illustrates the ability of a small independent to be flexible. There would be no chance of any of the big chains doing this for a demanding customer. Never doubt that there will always be room for the small independent establishment of character.**

To be able to provide such a selection you will almost certainly have had to:

◆ set up a team of specialist suppliers
◆ obtain goods from a cash and carry
◆ shop at a supermarket.

In addition you may well have cooked some food in your own house.

Let's consider them in turn and the kinds of issues raised in each case.

Specialist suppliers

Bread

In the bad old days customers might have been offered basic rolls or sliced white bread entirely devoid of flavour. Try this now and you won't last long. People expect sandwich bars to offer them an interesting choice which includes some at least from the following list (which is by no means exhaustive):

brown and white rolls, with and without sesame seeds or poppy seeds
bagels
walnut bread
baguettes of various sizes, brown as well as white
subs
ciabatta
focaccia
caramelised onion roll
naan bread
pain rustique
seeded *gallego*
organic sunflower bread

hazelnut and raisin *boule*
carcaca (Portuguese)
onion bread
apple and thyme rolls
baps
tomato bread
sliced bread: brown, white, rye, wholemeal.

You can even get chocolate bread! Assuming you want to offer, say, six or seven choices to your customers it is unlikely that you will find one bakery which can supply them all. This might be because they don't do them all or can't do them all to a high enough standard. We found it very frustrating that the people who could give us great sesame seed rolls made poor quality bagels or walnut bread.

Don't compromise for the sake of convenience.

It's a question of trial and error and it is most unlikely that the group of suppliers you start with will be the same six months later. The good news is that a settled pattern *will* emerge after a while. Engaging with and trying out new suppliers is a necessary process during which you must keep your critical faculties working *flat out*.

This way you ensure that the selection you offer is of the best quality available in your area.

Suppliers will naturally be very keen to do business with you. Take advantage of this by obtaining free samples from as many of them as possible. Ask to visit their premises; only people with something to hide will refuse such requests. By doing these things and getting to know them you will soon get an idea of which ones will fit in with your scheme of things. If you end up with surplus bread samples, stick them in the freezer at home and use them later.

Don't sell defrosted bread to the public.

Quite a lot of places do this. That's their choice. However, whilst it's OK for the home the quality is not as good as fresh – and there are plenty of customers who will be able to tell the difference. If you find you regularly have a lot of bread left over, reduce the amount you order rather than freezing what's left over to be sold the next day.

Remember also the benefits of a bake-off oven which I talked about in Chapter Five. It won't meet all your bread needs but it will probably serve to cut out one or two suppliers. It will also result in more control, less waste and some saving financially. Having said this it is best and simplest for baking baguettes. We have tried a number of other items such as croissants and savoury snacks – all have been more fiddly and less consistent.

Fruit and vegetables

As well as bread, every sandwich bar needs to have lettuce, cucumber and tomatoes right at the start of the day. For this you need a wholesale fruit and vegetable supplier who can deliver early in the morning. They can also provide you with fresh herbs, apples, oranges, lemons, grapefruits, avocados, vegetables for home-made soup and so on.

As with all suppliers you can get names and addresses from the *Yellow Pages*. In the case of fruit and vegetable suppliers it is not really appropriate to get samples since they all sell the same stuff. I recommend that you go and visit them and talk to them about your requirements. You need to satisfy yourself that the quality of their goods is of a high standard. I did this with our present supplier and indeed for a time collected the supplies myself. The air was filled with the worst language imaginable but somehow it didn't matter. More important was the sense of camaraderie and hard work which pervaded the place.

> **The main thing to watch out for with fruit and vegetables is not to order too much.**

Fruit and vegetables are highly perishable. It is not so much of a problem with lettuce, cucumber and tomatoes – you will go through a lot of them every day and indeed the problem might be running out. But in the case of avocados and apples, if you buy by the box, they will all ripen at about the same time. You can suddenly find yourself with 20 ripe avocados on the same day which will mean only one thing – waste. You should consider whether it is better to buy smaller quantities of such goods on a regular basis from your supermarket, which might deliver. Arrange such deliveries to coincide with your own shopping.

In the case of bread and fruit and vegetables there are two potentially problematic areas:

1. Honesty

The goods must be delivered before you arrive so you have to hand out keys. You might have a shop with a vestibule area so that the supplier simply has to open the outer door or roller shutter. If not, it means that the delivery person will have free access to your shop. Whilst the supplier is hardly going to jeopardise a regular order by stealing the odd chocolate bar it is possible to get the occasional new driver who is light-fingered. You really just have to monitor things, especially if you engage a new company to supply goods. I have never been aware of a problem and I really don't think there are many people who would risk their job for a chocolate bar or two.

I know one proprietor who will not give out a key under any circumstances. This means that bread, fruit, vegetables and sometimes milk are left in the street, possibly for as long as two hours. From a health and hygiene point of view I regard this as unacceptable.

2. Reliability

You simply cannot get going if the correct stuff isn't there when you arrive in the morning. And it must be of consistently good quality. There is nothing worse than trying to race about collecting bread or cucumbers in rush hour traffic while the staff twiddle their thumbs. Our first supplier of fruit and vegetables was a nightmare. The excuses for non-delivery included the following:

◆ the key to our shop was in the other van which was on a different run
◆ the key was in a van which was in the garage being repaired
◆ the key had temporarily gone missing
◆ the driver accidentally took the key home the night before and it was in his other trousers
◆ Uri Geller had been practising on the key. Actually I made that one up – but it got to the stage where nothing would have surprised me.

We put up with this nonsense for too long. Don't you make the same mistake. If it happens once, fair enough. If it happens again soon afterwards use somebody else. We have now had the same supplier for many years and they have hardly ever let us down.

Butchers and fishmongers

The question here is whether you use large suppliers or small independents. If you choose the former then in my view you will risk sacrificing quality. In the case of meat you will get a processed product – blocks of chicken or turkey 'formed from' a whole lot of bits of chickens or turkeys and tightly sealed in thick polythene. They will probably be highly salted. Things have improved in recent years as standards generally have gone up but I would say that fresh is still best.

In the case of fish it is arguably not so important because much of what you want will not be fresh – for instance, tuna, crabstick and prawns. It depends on the range you want to offer.

> We make our own fresh salmon mayonnaise which would be truly second rate if we used tinned salmon. We buy the salmon from a small local fish shop. For us, small independent is best in both cases.

Apart from anything else you develop a relationship with the people involved. You benefit from their expertise. They are more likely to be flexible and help out if you suddenly realise you've forgotten to order something. *After all, they're small business people too.*

If meat or fish are delivered to you they must be delivered at the right temperature. There are strict rules regarding the temperature for storing meat, fish and other items which you must observe. (I shall deal with this subject in Chapter Nine.) However, for the purposes of this chapter on suppliers remember that people who deliver such items to you must ensure that they reach you at the right temperature. Strictly speaking you should check that the temperatures are correct on arrival and keep a record. For checking temperatures you will need a probe thermometer. They cost about £25.

Cheese and milk

Since cheese keeps reasonably well it makes sense to save a little money by buying it in larger quantities from one of the bigger suppliers (subject always to having sufficient storage space). This also means that you will have some time before you have to pay for it – a perk not available at the supermarket. To make life easier we cut big blocks into smaller pieces, wrap them in cling film and store them in the fridge for future use. Do this during the afternoon when you're not under pressure so that you won't have to struggle with large blocks of cheese when you are.

The really important thing about milk is getting it into the fridge right away.

It's 10.15 on a warm summer's morning. You're thinking you really must speak to someone about air-conditioning for the shop. It's quite busy. There are a few people sitting drinking milkshakes and coffees. You're chatting to a customer. The milk delivery guy arrives late, looking harassed. He mumbles an apology, dumps a crate with three dozen cartons of milk on the floor somewhere near the fridge and rushes out. The conversation with the customer is very interesting. A group of students arrive wanting sandwiches made up. While you're doing that the lunchtime rush starts early. Just after one o'clock you suddenly notice the crate of milk. Panic stations. You now have a queue. You see a customer holding a carton of milk which he has obviously just picked out of the crate...

Try to get your delivery person to put the milk straight into the fridge. If they don't, make sure you do. Also make sure that you rotate the milk and that the sell-by date is obvious to the customer. If you don't do this you will have the irritating spectacle of people bending down into the refrigerated display unit, fiddling about with the cartons and probably disorganising other things. It is an offence to sell goods which are past their sell-by dates.

Pre-prepared sandwich fillings

There are many suppliers who can provide you with a variety of exotic-sounding fillings in plastic boxes: chicken tikka, Mexican chicken with red kidney beans, Thai prawn mayonnaise, etc. There's no doubt they are convenient. You just take the lid off, plonk the box down in your deli serve-over and scoop out the appropriate measure. They're usually heavy with mayonnaise-type sauces and are generally easy to work with.

In fact they're good from every point of view except flavour!

I admit that I'm biased. I don't like them. I think they always have that processed flavour. It's hardly surprising given that they have been turned out in massive quantities, with a variety of additives and preservatives, in a factory somewhere. No matter how you try you simply cannot reproduce fresh natural flavours and textures in this way. To my way of thinking they also lack individual character – something of a problem if you are trying to stand out in the crowd as a small independent. It's easier for the large chains to do this well; because of their buying power they can negotiate direct with a supplier to ensure a level of individuality and quality for their sandwich fillings. You, on the other hand, will simply have to take what the large national operations have to offer at any particular time.

If this kind of thing does appeal to you – and the convenience and lack of waste factors are considerable – do check with as many suppliers as possible and get as many free samples as your fridge will hold – happy tasting!

Coffee and tea

'The secret of life is a good cup of coffee.' So sang a thoughtful singer-songwriter called Gretchen Peters a few years ago. Coffee has become a kind of religion for a lot of people nowadays – one with its own language. Consider this order placed recently by a customer in London:

'A double, no fun, skinny, vente, dry, capp to-go.' Translated this means 20oz of no fat (skinny) milk poured onto two measures of decaffeinated (no fun) espresso coffee with more foam and less milk (dry) in a paper cup to take away.

> Unbelievably, when we opened our first sandwich bar in the mid-nineties we only sold filter coffee – you know, the kind that stews in a pyrex jug. We soon realised that the continental taste for a range of freshly brewed coffees was spreading like wildfire. We invested in a compact machine which allowed us to produce bean to cup espresso, cappuccino and latte as well as various flavoured coffees, all individually made to order.

You can buy coffee from the cash and carry or indeed the supermarket but I think it is better to go to a specialist supplier for the following reasons:

◆ You can make savings by buying in bulk (coffee which is properly packaged and stored will keep for a considerable length of time: 18 months to two years).
◆ You benefit from their expertise and experience. They should be happy and willing to arrange tasting sessions to allow you to pick one or more coffees which are right for you.
◆ A specialist supplier will probably be able to advise you on suitable coffee machines for your size of operation. In addition they should be able to supply and maintain such equipment.
◆ Specialists are aware of new trends and fashions in this increasingly popular area, and pass them on to you.

Despite the numerous outlets selling good quality coffee nowadays industry surveys suggest that there is still a large number of people ready and waiting to be introduced to the delights of the real thing. Incredibly, some people still drink instant coffee!

Good quality coffee is absolutely essential.

Tea is a different kettle of fish, so to speak. Most places use tea bags. You can obtain a range, from bog standard to top notch, at the cash and carry. The profit margin on a cup of tea is substantial, so use the best tagged tea bags you can get; and do offer a decent selection. Many people nowadays know the difference between Earl Grey, Darjeeling and Assam. Offer a range of herbal or fruit teas (again, all available in bags). It won't cost much but it will enable you to offer an impressive choice to the customer.

You may decide to go one better and provide individual pots of leaf tea. I salute you if you do. In this case I think you will be best to use a specialist supplier for the reasons stated previously on the subject of coffee. Indeed your coffee supplier will almost certainly supply tea too.

I think there is real scope for expansion in the field of tea. Historically it has been the most popular drink in Britain but now it has become the poor relation. Whilst people will go to great lengths to provide a perfect cup of coffee most still think it's quite sufficient to pour boiling water over a tea bag – tagged if you're lucky. You are rarely if ever offered a choice of full fat or semi-skimmed milk. And what about the delights of Earl Grey, Darjeeling, lemon tea, frappés (iced teas blended with fruit), herb and flavoured teas and so on?

There is more work in producing individual pots of leaf tea, but no more than in providing decent coffee. And you can make tea in cafetiéres. I really do believe that tea can be a growth area. I understand that some outlets have opened in recent times which do specialise in providing a range of good quality teas. Indeed there was a Typhoo tea bar in the Millennium Dome. But this is a drop in the ocean when compared to the culture which has brought good quality coffee to countless catering outlets the length and breadth of the country.

There are also interesting tea products from abroad, most notably chai. This is a concoction of black India teas, honey and aromatic spices. It can be blended with milk to produce a chai latte drink. Chai comes either in powdered or concentrate form.

Water quality
There's not a lot of point in sourcing top quality tea and coffee unless the water they're made with tastes good too. The hardness of water in the UK varies considerably. The harder the water the harsher the taste of drinks produced with it. Given that 99% of most drinks is water this can be a serious issue. If you are in a hard water area you should

seriously consider acquiring a water filter which can improve water quality by removing unpleasant elements, thus allowing the natural flavour to come through. Such filters also help to prevent the formation of scale and this in turn reduces the risk of limescale damage to your equipment. Your catering supply company will be able to advise you on suppliers of filters in your area.

Some general points to note on the subject of suppliers:

◆ When looking for suppliers, spread the net wide at the start. If you taste something you really like at another sandwich-coffee bar, ask the owner who his supplier is. Other than that it's a case of trawling the internet, *Yellow Pages* and *International Sandwich and Snack News*.

◆ In the case of small independent suppliers don't choose ones which are too far away. If their van breaks down they might not have any back-up and you might have to go and collect the stuff yourself. Equally, satisfy yourself that they can deliver reliably at times which suit you.

◆ Always try to negotiate some level of discount from any supplier to whom you give regular business. Having said that, once you have agreed a price that you are both happy with, don't seek further reductions unless there is a change of circumstances, such as you ordering other products or increasing your order significantly because you open another outlet. You want to have a good relationship and constantly trying to get the price down for no particular reason will not help to achieve this.

◆ Always be on the look-out for new ideas from existing and new suppliers. The catering industry is always coming up with new products. Check in *International Sandwich and Snack News* where a lot of them advertise and which often features appraisals of new products. Visit other sandwich-coffee bars from time to time and see what they're up to.

◆ Don't have any qualms whatever about taking free samples from as many people as possible. You will find when you open you will be targeted by lots of roving reps. Fill up your fridge and freezer; it's a perk of the job and you might just come across something good.

◆ *Always, but especially when starting out, check that what is delivered is exactly what was ordered and that everything including the packaging is in good order.* If anything is wrong or damaged, don't accept it. The delivery driver may complain but if you do this at the start the message will quickly get through that you are businesslike. You will thus be far less likely to experience problems in the future. Check also that you are not being given goods which are close to their sell-by dates.

◆ You should send a pro-forma letter to all suppliers asking them to confirm *in writing* that their operation complies with all relevant food hygiene regulations and that they have in place an appropriate system of Hazard Analysis Critical Control Point (HACCP). (See Chapter Nine for more information on this.) All you are really doing is getting them to confirm that they are doing what the law requires them to do. Obtaining such letters achieves the twin aims of reassuring you and also demonstrating that you have taken all reasonable steps to comply with legal requirements. Apart from anything else this might be helpful in the unlikely event of any claim being made against you.

◆ Arrange tasting sessions with some of your friends or relations. This is a particularly good idea when you are starting out and have lots of free samples. You are so overloaded with things to do that you will find it difficult to make time to assess the merits of different brands of coffee, juice or whatever – a vital task. An objective point of view can be very useful indeed – the benefits of a focus group!

◆ Having a lot of suppliers inevitably leads to a lot of paperwork. Apart from being well organised and having a good filing system consider internet banking – it's becoming more popular and soon I believe it will be commonplace for even small businesses to pay bills online. This saves writing out cheques, addressing envelopes (though your PC can be set up to do this) and buying stamps.

Also, set up pro-forma order forms on your computer and print them out when necessary. This means you don't have to hunt about for scraps of paper at four o'clock in the afternoon to write lists on. It also means that you don't actually write anything, you just tick the items you need.

◆ When you start to order goods from larger suppliers they might want cash on delivery. This should only be until they have set up a credit account which will involve obtaining a bank reference. If you can arrange this before you start trading, all to the good – it's not convenient to have to take large amounts of cash out of the till to pay suppliers. If they arrive in the morning they'll use up most of your float.

Non-food items

Up until now I have talked about suppliers of food products. Whilst these are very important don't overlook non-food items.

1. Cleaning materials

This includes floor cleaner, washing up liquid, residual sanitiser (to be sprayed over surfaces last thing at night), cloths, paper towel dispensers, paper towels and so on. A lot of the things under this heading can of course be bought from the supermarket or the cash and carry. However, it might be advantageous to buy them from specialist suppliers in larger, commercial quantities. They will deliver to you and once you have an account with them you have a degree of control over when you pay them. They may also be cheaper than the supermarket or cash and carry. They will also be able to give you advice on new products coming onto the market.

2. Lightbulbs

The cost of some halogen spotlights can be frightening. For our second shop we had a hanging strip of spotlights installed above the food prep area. Absolutely wonderful – until I found that the cheapest price in Edinburgh for one replacement bulb (the strip has ten spotlights) was over £11! Fortunately I then discovered a specialist mail order company which sold the same bulbs for under £4. Not only that but their prices for the many other light bulbs were highly competitive; and on orders of £50 or more, next day delivery was free. *As they say, it pays to shop around.*

3. Packaging

Packaging is very important from both the aesthetic and practical points of view. Take coffee cups. Clearly they have to keep the coffee hot – but they should also be easy to drink out of when you are walking along the street. Hence the desirability of sip lids which allow you to drink tea or coffee without having to fiddle about with two hands taking the lid off and then replacing it.

With cold drinks such as fruit smoothies or milkshakes it's more important to see what's inside – the colours are so nicely garish! So polystyrene won't do; it has to be clear. The lid should be made in such a way that you can push a straw through a hole in the top.

For sliced bread sandwiches you want triangular plastic boxes which will hold sandwiches made with your preferred kind of bread. The correct size is vital; a sandwich made with thick sliced bread and lots of lettuce will not fit into every such box.

For salads you will need a clear plastic box possibly with a 'spork' attached (a cross between a spoon and a fork). Bear in mind also that you must get the size of box which fits in with your notion of how much salad you plan to include in one portion. A half-filled box does not look like good value.

> **Make sure you get some samples of plastic containers and try them out for size before you order lots. You usually have to buy these containers in large quantities so it's important to do your homework in advance and ensure you don't end up with 5,000 containers that you can't use.**

A company that specialises in packaging will probably be able to provide you with carrier bags (and also coffee cups) with your logo on the side.

As with everything else, think it through well in advance. You don't want to be scrambling about looking for the right size of sandwich bag the day before you open.

4. Stationery

Clearly you can buy paper and pens from numerous outlets. However, as with light bulbs there are specialist mail order firms which will supply every conceivable stationery need at prices well below those in your local shops. This can be particularly relevant if you are going to print your own menus, notices, staff handbooks, temperature charts and order forms; you will go through prodigious amounts of paper. Again you have the benefit of ordering goods but not paying for them for a few weeks. Credit cards are generally acceptable. Delivery is usually free if your order is above a certain amount (generally around £30.)

Paying bills

I hope I haven't given the impression that opening accounts with suppliers is a licence to avoid making payments. You will come across small-business people who think that good credit control means ordering things and then not paying for them until legal proceedings are about to begin. I deplore this attitude. It is both selfish and short-sighted, because suppliers will simply refuse to have anything to do with people who do this. Conversely if you usually pay your bills within a reasonable time suppliers will be flexible if, for instance, you hit a quiet period and need some extra time to pay.

> **It also overlooks the fact that suppliers, particularly the smaller ones, are in exactly the same boat as you – they need the money to make their world go round just as much as you do.**

Used sensibly, credit accounts with suppliers are beneficial because you have some degree of control over when you make payment. They also mean that you only have to make a payment once every week or fortnight for example.

No matter how small your business might be you will find yourself dealing with a considerable number of suppliers. Finding the right combination of suppliers for your operation will take time. In fact the process never really stops. One firm might go out of business, another might put it's prices up prompting you to switch to another one recommended by a friend.

> **In addition to the specialists you will need to use the services**
> **of a cash and carry and a supermarket.**

Using a cash and carry

Cash and carry wholesalers are not all the same. When you have a good idea of the sorts of ingredients you will require for the sandwiches you intend to sell, go and visit a few in your area. They will be happy to show you round. Pick one that seems to have a lot of the things you will regularly need such as:

mayonnaise
drinks
tea bags
chocolate and other sweet bars
ice-creams
baking ingredients such as nuts (if you intend to do any home-baking)
chewing gum
plastic spoons
pickles
crisps
biscuits
tortilla wraps

Try to make sure they have a selection of things beyond the routine and the well known – this will allow you to try out new things from time to time.

Before a cash and carry will allow you to buy things you will have to register with them. This usually involves them taking up bank and trade references. When starting up, trade references can present obvious difficulties. You will have to satisfy them that you have started in business in the sense that you have a business bank account, headed paper or indeed some invoices addressed to your business. This will set you apart from Joe Public in their eyes. Initially you might have to make payments in cash until a trading pattern has been established.

Try to organise things so that you only need to go to the cash and carry once a week. They are usually open long hours so you should be able to go at a time most convenient to you.

Despite this, loading up a trolley at the cash and carry is a bit of a chore. Some cash and carries will make it easier by loading up your order for you. To do this they will usually require a faxed order the day before. They can even put it all through their till but leave it untotalled. This way if you want to add on something else when you get there you can.

> **Always be on the look-out for ways of making your life that little bit easier. Over the course of a year they really do add up.**

Buying from supermarkets

Why do you need to buy things from a supermarket when you're dealing with so many suppliers? The fact is there will always be some things which it's better and cheaper to buy from supermarkets.

Soon after we opened we decided to introduce a bagel with taramasalata and seedless grapes. I assumed we could get taramasalata from the cash and carry or from a specialist delicatessen supplier. We did get some but it was utterly disgusting – and we had to buy two dozen jars at a time: far more than we needed. We were left with no alternative but to buy it from the supermarket – in quantities that suited us. Similarly, we did not need many seedless grapes and it would have been inappropriate to order one small bag from our wholesale fruit and vegetable supplier.

There are many other similar examples when you want to buy smallish quantities of reliably good quality items. For instance:

- **Avocados:** notoriously difficult to get just right for sandwiches. Buy a few regularly and your customers, like ours, will marvel at your ability to serve them up consistently with the correct degree of ripeness.
- **Tinned olives: black, green, sliced, pitted** – it's unlikely that you will want to fill up a lot of your valuable storage space with boxes full of these things.
- **Pastrami:** we have an excellent butcher but the one thing he doesn't seem to able to produce consistently is pastrami – but our supermarket can.
- **Tinned strawberries and raspberries for fruit smoothies:** if you buy large catering tins from the cash and carry and the weather suddenly turns nasty you find yourself with the challenge of trying to keep a lot of tinned strawberries and raspberries fresh. They will take up space in the fridge and might pick up other, less appealing, flavours. Raspberry and smoked mackerel? I don't think so.
- **Apples, oranges and bananas:** as I mentioned before if you buy a whole box of these from your wholesaler they will all be ready at around about the same time and if they don't sell, it's wasteful. At the supermarket you can take the quantity you need and ensure good quality.

There are many other examples. Frustratingly you will find that even the supermarket doesn't fill every gap. You will probably find yourself ordering certain of the more obscure drinks, as well as some vegetarian patés or houmous or trendy little tray-bakes from small or large specialist suppliers.

By the way: if you're comparing prices at the cash and carry with those at the supermarket remember that prices marked on the cash and carry shelves don't include VAT.

Supplying yourself

There are two ways of doing this, from cooking facilities either in your shop or in your house.

I have already talked about the complications of installing full-scale cooking facilities in your shop: architects, planning application, ventilation, time, money and so on. There are advantages, however, not least the fact that production is all contained within your business unit, so you don't need to take your work home with you.

If you don't want the expense and trouble of what this involves, there is another option: namely doing some cooking at home. There are a number of advantages:

◆ **You can produce quality items which are unique to you.** Take the case of chocolate cake. You can go into any one of hundreds of sandwich-coffee bars and be served exactly the same kinds – often mass produced in a factory and full of additives to increase shelf life. Alternatively, you can find a really good recipe and make it yourself. Customers will come to appreciate the difference. And there's no ordering or invoicing involved.

◆ **You can save money.** You buy ingredients in bulk from the cash and carry and don't have to pay somebody else to do the actual baking or cooking.

◆ **You can prepare food in batches at times that suit you.** You then freeze it ready for later use. Do remember to mark the date on frozen items; to ensure the quality is maintained I do not recommend freezing anything for much over a month. Always remember: first in, first out.

◆ **It's the kind of activity that could be fitted round a part-time job.** If you or your partner want to maintain a job but also make a useful contribution to the new business, preparing food in the house at flexible times could be the perfect thing.

However, it's not all plain sailing.

In general terms the food hygiene and health and safety rules are the same as those applicable to your shop. These are dealt with in Chapter Nine. There are particular points which apply in the case of food preparation at home:

◆ You can't carry out 'domestic activities' which might present a risk of food contamination at the same time as you prepare food for the shop. This includes handling laundry. I have in fact been told by an environmental health officer that you should not prepare food for the shop in a kitchen containing a washing machine.

◆ Pets must be kept out at all times.

◆ There must be effective separation in your fridge of items for the home and those for the shop.

◆ You may conceivably have to stop cooking in the house if any member of your household contracts an infectious disease.

◆ When you deliver food from house to shop the correct temperature limits (see Chapter Nine) should be observed. If your shop is a considerable distance from your house, this might mean having to acquire a refrigerated van.

◆ Food surfaces must be cleaned and disinfected regularly.

While it may be possible to observe these rules in your home kitchen you have to admit it won't be easy – especially if you have children (particularly teenagers) and cats or dogs. It would be a great deal easier if you could create a second kitchen in your house. This would of course result in not inconsiderable expenditure. You have to decide how important it is to your plans.

Bear in mind also that health inspectors have the legal right to inspect the premises after giving one day's notice. Do you like the idea of them poking around your kitchen?

My wife and I have created a second kitchen in our house purely for the shop – and very successful it has been, too. We prepare grilled, barbecued and curried chicken breasts, bacon, boiled eggs, salmon, aubergine caviar, soup and cakes. We like to think our ability to produce items with our own recipes gives us something of an edge over our competitors. The only drawback has been at holiday time. If we want the shop to continue operating while we are away it means someone has to come into the house and prepare food and then transport it to the shop. Nothing is ever simple!

CHAPTER SEVEN

Fitting Out and Equipping the Shop

Timing is crucial

Good timing is vital because it helps to keep the costs down.

You agree a deal on March 1st whereby you will get the keys to your dream shop unit on May 1st. You work really hard during March and April getting quotes, choosing suppliers, planning the layout and buying and ordering equipment. You've worked out that it will take a month to fit out the shop after you get the keys. You provisionally plan an opening party for June 1st. The trouble is there's one little job you kept putting off: ordering the refrigerated display unit which will contain your made-up sandwiches, salads and drinks. You eventually get round to it in the second last week of April. Your supplier looks a little taken aback when you say you want to open on June 1st but says it should just be possible. A mild panic sets in at the back of your mind, but you're so busy with other things…

A few days after you get the keys on May 1st your fridge man phones to say that the dairy unit, which is being built in Italy, might be delayed. There's been some industrial relations problem at the factory and they're now talking about a delivery date of mid June *or thereabouts*.

Panic now strikes. Suddenly all the other things that you've been attending to so efficiently are forgotten. Every thinking moment is filled with despairing visions of bolshy Italian trade unionists and idle factory production lines in Milan.

As June 1st looms ever larger it seems that everything else will be ready on time. But you can't open without a dairy unit. So what do you do? Cancel the order and try desperately to get another one from somewhere else, a second-hand one perhaps? And what about the staff who are expecting to start on June 1st? And didn't you assure the bank manager that by the end of the first week in June the money would be starting to flow the other way?

OK I'm laying it on a bit thick, but only a bit. And the dairy unit is only one example of the kind of thing that could delay the commencement of trading; there are lots more.

So, whilst you can plan things in a reasonably leisurely way in the early stages, once you agree a deal and dates become set in stone everything changes. Whether it's suppliers of fridges or coffee-making machines, electricians, signwriters or plumbers it's vital to get clear assurances on likely time scales. 'When can you start?', 'How long will it take?' and 'When can you deliver it?' will become your personal mantras.

Once you've gone beyond the point of no return your overarching objective must be to keep to an absolute minimum the time between the day you get the keys and the day you start trading.

It's one of the oldest truisms in the book: time is money.

Shopfitters versus individual tradespeople

Clearly this is an important decision which must be taken early on. If you decide to use a firm of shopfitters there are obvious advantages:

◆ They will co-ordinate the various trades, particularly electrician, plumber, carpenter and decorator. You will only have to talk to one or two people from one organisation, not lots of individual workers.

◆ You will (or certainly should) have a written agreement which will tie them down to a particular completion date, ideally with penalties for failure to complete on time. Having said that, there will be some get-out clauses to cover them in the event of unforeseeable problems once they start pulling up floorboards.

◆ Assuming you select the right company for your particular needs, you will get the benefit of their experience of fitting out similar units in the past. They will probably come up with good ideas on layout, the most durable materials for food prep surfaces and so on.

However, using shopfitters will not be right for everyone. It's an expensive option.

Some years ago we were interested in a small unit (about 500 square feet) in the city centre. It was in shell condition. We asked a firm of shopfitters to give us an idea of likely costs. They were only talking about some stripping out, electrics, plumbing, joinery work and decoration. The 'basic' cost quoted was £10,000. It was made clear that this was a very rough figure which would almost certainly be exceeded. This did not include any equipment, floor coverings, light fittings or signs. As I watched the man driving off in the latest BMW I was pretty sure that we would not use shopfitters. After all, I was still going to have to deal with and co-ordinate a number of other people so why not a few more? – particularly when it would mean avoiding spending rather a lot of money. I concluded that in our case shopfitters would be an unaffordable luxury.

It really depends on your circumstances. If you are planning a sizeable operation and you have enough money at your disposal then using shopfitters makes sense. The bigger chains wouldn't consider anything else – but they will have worked out a deal with one particular company whereby in exchange for a lot of work (carried out in the shortest possible time), the price will be kept low.

This illustrates one of the problems of the small business which I have alluded to before. A lot of companies and organisations prefer dealing with larger customers. Small business owners, sadly, often find that they simply don't have much clout.

One compromise would be to co-ordinate everything yourself at the outset but plan to use shopfitters to revamp the place three years down the line on the assumption that things are going well. By that stage your bank will be happy to provide the necessary finance.

Whatever you decide, you should obtain quotes from at least two firms and make sure that they are used to carrying out contracts for operations of your size.

If you take over an existing business and you don't intend to do much beyond re-decorating the unit and making slight alterations to the layout then, of course, shopfitters won't be necessary.

If you decide *not* to use shopfitters there are a number of key points to bear in mind:

◆ **Get the ball rolling sooner rather than later.** Whether it's a quote from the decorators, the floorlayers or the electricians, start things moving as quickly as possible. This way you will create a bit of room for manoeuvre later on if and when problems arise. You should ideally have reached the stage of accepting quotations for the major works approximately eight to ten weeks before your planned opening.
◆ **Be organised and always think a bit ahead.** You should always be aware of what's coming up. And don't keep it all in your head. Have a do list, a timetable or a flow chart – whatever works for you – and update it on a daily (hourly in the last few days) basis.
◆ **Get quotes – including the terms of any guarantees – in writing wherever possible.** It doesn't mean that everything is sure to be problem-free but what you've agreed to is there in black and white – and you have a much greater prospect of some meaningful comeback in the event of later disputes.

◆ **Be very wary of using friends or friends of friends.** I know it's often financially tempting to do this but it's fraught with difficulty. You'll inevitably have a less professional approach with them and may well feel awkward about insisting on having things in writing. They might treat your project as one which they can fit round their main job. If things go wrong you'll find it harder to complain and you might jeopardise your friendship.

◆ **Co-ordinate the tasks carefully.** Don't have the decorators booked for a time when the joiners will be using an electric saw and creating lots of dust. This really can be a challenge and there will probably be times when you'll wish you had used shopfitters.

◆ **Be prepared to take a hard line if necessary.** Let's say the electrician confirms he will be at the shop all day Thursday to finish the re-wiring. Then he phones on Wednesday to say he can't make Thursday after all because of some other job which has gone on longer than expected. You know the decorator is planning to start on Friday and it doesn't suit you to have the electrician working that day.

> **Not for the last time you will have to be assertive in a situation you probably don't feel especially trained to meet. This is the lot of the small businessman. The good news is it gets easier with practice.**

◆ **Try to defer payment of your start-up costs.** One of the frightening aspects of this stage is the number of substantial bills you incur. And the total always seems to come to more than you originally estimated. Obviously your finance should be in place by this stage, but the longer it is until you draw down some or all of the funds the longer it will be until you incur liability for significant amounts of interest. Or if you're paying some of the bills out of savings the longer you will go on earning interest. And the greater the chances that you will be generating some reasonable income when the time comes to meet the payments.

Nothing I say here should be interpreted as advice to not pay bills until the very last minute. However, if you speak to companies early on you might well find they are prepared to accept a slightly later than usual payment date.

◆ **Set up a filing system that works for you.** You just can't imagine the frustration which is caused by being unable to lay your hands on an important quotation, specification or other vital document when you really need it. It's best to have everything in duplicate. Scan all important documents into your PC. Have a list with the names and phone numbers of everybody involved in the project with day and, if possible, evening phone numbers. *Have a copy of this list and your mobile phone with you at all times.*

Whether you use shopfitters or not, remember that if you need to apply to your local authority for planning permission to change the use of the premises and/or permission to move sinks around, knock down internal walls or create doorways, any such applications will take a considerable time to be decided, even assuming there are no hitches. This can mean delays before some of the work can be started. It all has to be factored into the equation. The time scales will vary from place to place – it is impossible to be categorical. Check with the planning and building control departments at your local council offices – or your architect.

Involving the environmental health officer

I mentioned in Chapter Two the desirability of consulting your local EHO prior to concluding a deal. It also makes sense to involve them when you have started, or are just about to start, fitting out the shop. You should have detailed plans for them to look at. Go over these to check for any pitfalls.

Here's a true life example of the benefits of doing this:

When we were fitting out our first shop I invited our EHO to visit. He pointed out that where we intended to put one set of electrical sockets was too close to one of the sinks. We had already carried out some of the work but it was still quite a straightforward matter to alter our plans and move the sockets. If we had waited until the first inspection after we had started trading then we would have been involved in a lot of work which would have caused considerable disruption and greatly hampered our ability to trade. It would have also used up money which we could have ill-afforded.

Buying equipment

If you take over a business as a going concern it may be well endowed with good quality modern equipment. In this case you will be spared one major job associated with setting up a brand new sandwich-coffee bar.

However, catering equipment does have a limited lifespan because of the constant and hard wear to which it is subjected six or seven days a week. Some of the items you acquire from the previous owner will soon be coming up for replacement.

If you are starting from scratch you will have to buy everything from freezers to knives. In some ways this is advantageous:

◆ you get to choose things which you prefer as opposed to things which somebody else took a notion to a few years previously and which might now look dated. Nowadays items such as serve-overs and dairy units come in many designs. Since such things will have a prominent place at the heart of your shop it's good to have something you like and feel comfortable with – and which will impress the customers.

◆ in the case of the larger items you get guarantees so that for a year at least you know that if something breaks down somebody else will sort it out.

> **Remember also that if you can buy as many items as possible from one particular supplier you will have considerable scope for negotiating a decent discount.**

As a general rule always buy new equipment – *and keep the manuals and all of the guarantee documentation together in a readily accessible place.* Apart from the points mentioned previously, you don't know if second-hand equipment has been well looked after. Will it let you down after a month or two? Bear in mind also that you probably won't get any worthwhile guarantee.

On the other hand, there is a market for second-hand fridges, coffee-making machines, dairy units, etc. You might be lucky and get good ones in which case you will certainly save money. If you do go for second-hand, try to buy from a reputable dealer – preferably someone with whom you, or someone you trust, has had previous dealings.

> **But ask yourself: which would you prefer for your kitchen at home – new or second-hand?**

Let's consider various points about some of the main pieces of equipment you will need.

Serve-over, dairy unit, fridge, freezer

These four constitute the basic minimum requirement for the storage of food products and the display of sandwiches and salads. You might also have a display fridge for drinks and a display freezer for ice cream. Ideally you should choose a shop unit which allows for the installation of more such equipment in the future when you've become so popular that you need more space to store and display your increasing selection of wares.

Serve-over. This really is central to the operation. Sometimes referred to as a delicatessen unit, it displays the meats, cheeses, mayonnaises, salads, olives, houmous, etc. which will be used to make up your sandwiches. Customers are naturally drawn to it. They usually stand there while they talk to you or your staff and give their order.

It follows that it must be kept sparkling clean at all times. In addition the food displayed should always be in first class condition and order. Don't display bowls of tuna mayonnaise with just a little bit left and smears of dried out stuff encrusted round the edge. Even when it's busy you should try to get into the habit of neatening up bowls of mayonnaise or trays of meat once you have taken what you need for a particular sandwich.

A word of advice which could save you money and hassle: I don't know what it is about serve-overs but customers often see them as counters which they can lean on. I really don't understand this since they're the wrong shape and the wrong height. The danger is that they might crack the glass. Serve-overs invariably have large sections of curved glass and if they do crack it causes real problems.

> This happened to us once. We had to clear out all the food because of the risk that particles of glass might have got into the food. We then had to order a replacement glass from Italy. It took five or six weeks to arrive during which time we had to rig up a sheet of polythene – you can imagine how good that looked.

Take great care when cleaning the glass. It is often the case that the glass can be opened out to allow access for cleaning. However, in this position it is very vulnerable. It's best either to find a way of cleaning it without doing this or ensuring that every member of staff understands the importance of handling it delicately.

Dairy unit/open-fronted refrigerated display unit. This is the other unit which customers are drawn to. It displays the pre-prepared sandwiches and might also be where you display a range of other things as well: salads, drinks, yoghurts, sushi. In summer you might also keep chocolate bars, fruit and cakes here.

In the past such units were very plain and all looked roughly the same. Things are very different now. I first realised this in the early-nineties when my wife and I visited London and looked at one of the early Pret A Manger units. Walking in there was a bit like entering the galley on the *Starship Enterprise*. It was all stainless steel and bright with subtle lighting.

Whether we like it or not, image is very important nowadays. When selecting your dairy unit go for quality, but choose one that looks good as well.

For our second shop we chose a serve-over and a dairy unit which featured matching royal blue strips along the front as well as a blue grill over the condenser. It doesn't make them any more efficient but they do look smart.

Fridges and freezers. The important point here is *not to be tempted to skimp by buying domestic equipment.* You will probably be horrified at how much more expensive the commercial fridges and freezers are – but they're worth it. You are paying for materials and build quality which make them able to withstand the rigours of commercial life. Quite apart from anything else a commercial fridge is opened and closed far more frequently than a domestic one.

> Take the chest freezer in our shop. We get deliveries of frozen baguettes two or three times a week. They come in boxes of 24 – just imagine how heavy they are. They are dumped without ceremony into the freezer. In addition we regularly buy fairly large tubs of ice-cream for milk-shakes. A domestic freezer just wouldn't stand up to this treatment for long without giving problems.

It's the same with fridges. We do in fact use a domestic fridge in the shop kitchen in our house. The pressure is not so intense but we often find that the little fittings holding the shelves in place break because they are just not designed to support the weight of large quantities of food.

You may want to have an upright display fridge purely for holding drinks: cans, bottles and cartons. These are particularly good in the summer. They have a door (glass-fronted) so that the drinks are kept as cool as possible. Before you invest a lot of money, check with some of the large companies to see if there are any deals on offer.

> When we started out Snapple had a major campaign in Britain. The deal was that they would give you a free display fridge (admittedly with a large Snapple sign on both sides) if you agreed to stock 60% of the available space with their products. That was a long time ago. We haven't heard from them for years but we still have the fridge.

You will also find that some companies will sell you fridges advertising their products at very favourable prices.

> **Never forget that you have something which is desirable to the big companies – advertising space in the high street. Always be on the look-out for ways to exploit this.**

Practical Points

◆ Always clean the condensers regularly. An old toothbrush is ideal. There are also sprays which eliminate the collected dust. Condensers are a bit like radiators in car engines. They suck in air but in the process they suck in a lot of dust which collects on them. If you do not clear this regularly – once a month is usually about right, but more often if necessary – then the condenser unit simply breaks down. This means you lose the use of a vital piece of equipment and also that you incur a cost running into several hundred pounds to replace the damaged unit.

◆ Find out where the condenser is before you have a unit installed. This is particularly important in the case of the serve-over and the dairy unit since they are difficult to move once installed. The condenser in our first unit was hard up against a wall. I only realised the significance of this when I first tried to clean it. Fortunately there was a small gap between the wall and the condenser. In order to clean it I had to writhe about on the floor like a potholer in a tight spot to get close enough to clean it. I reckon the supplier should have alerted me to this. But he didn't. Be warned.

◆ Before you confirm an order for any of the larger units, check that it will definitely go through the door to your shop. We had one unit which we only just managed to get into the shop after taking the front door off its hinges. This kind of thing creates a lot of stress – something you can well do without when you are trying to get your new business underway!

Coffee-making machine

In days gone by this would have been a very minor part of the equation.

> **Now it's quite simple – make it a priority and get the best machine you can afford.**

For the most basic 'bean to cup' machine (not plumbed in) capable of delivering good quality, individually prepared cups of espresso, cappuccino and café latte you will pay over £1,000. At the other end of the scale you could pay well over £20,000 for a top-of-the-range automatic machine.

Automatic machines are hugely appealing because they are simple to operate. Authentic coffee-making machines such as you see in Italy look and sound great but staff will have to be trained to get the best out of them. There is a considerable degree of skill required to turn out consistently excellent coffee.

> **The better the machine you get the more impressed the customers will be.**
> **Put simply – it will look and act the part. And what's more it will**
> **be robust and well able to stand up to heavy use.**

Do remember that any such machine *must* be thoroughly cleaned on a daily basis in accordance with the manufacturer's instructions. If you don't do this then oily residues build up in the pipes and the coffee you serve will have a bitter taste.

When making a purchase make sure that the supplier will be willing and able to send someone to demonstrate its correct use to you and your staff after it has been installed.

Contact grill

A contact grill is basically two heated plates which go together a bit like the two sides of a brief-case. You raise the top half with a heat resistant handle, put the sandwich on the bottom half and then lower the top half which rests on the sandwich – you don't need to push it down hard. We usually turn ours on in the morning and leave it on until after the lunch time rush. This way you don't need to waste time waiting for it to heat up.

For quite a lot of people the difference between a cheese and tomato sandwich and a *toasted* cheese and tomato sandwich is akin to that between a Ford Escort and a Rolls Royce. You might be surprised at the number of sandwich combinations which are amenable to being toasted. The things to avoid are the ones which include mayonnaise because it is just too liquid and drips everywhere. The contact grill can also be used for wraps.

These grills are sometimes referred to as 'Panini' grills after the name of a particular manufacturer. It is possible to buy pre-prepared and/or frozen sandwiches specifically designed for use in a Panini-style grill. It's a very compact item yet it adds considerably to the variety you can offer customers.

As with the coffee machine it is important to clean it regularly. You do this by scraping off the various bits of carbonised bread which accumulate in the course of the day – you will be provided with a scraper for this purpose.

Boiler

Nothing whatever to do with central heating, a boiler provides you with constant boiling water. Some coffee machines will provide this facility. Either way the unit should be plumbed in. Apart from making tea it's a handy source of hot water for cleaning the floor at the end of the day.

Soup kettle

Soup is a perennial favourite. Demand can drop off quite a bit during the summer but given the kinds of summers we normally experience in this country people still seem to feel the need for something hot.

Go for good build quality – i.e. the more expensive ones. They look better and they last longer.

> I have to confess that when we needed a new soup kettle a couple of years ago we went for a cheap one (£199). Superficially it looked OK but it was fiddly to use, and just after the guarantee expired the element burnt out. You live and learn (but the lessons just go on and on).

Lighting

Don't get hanging strip lights. If you take over an existing business which has them, get rid of them. They might be all right for providing light in an office or warehouse but they are far too basic and dated for a modern sandwich-coffee bar with any pretensions to style.

The imaginative use of light can add considerably to the atmosphere in the public area: side lights, chandeliers, uplighters, downlighters, picture lights etc. They also have practical uses. They can light up specific items such as the menu and thus make it easier to read regardless of the state of the weather outside. By shining a spot on a particular display you will draw attention to it and perhaps enhance sales.

It is different in the back area, in particular the food prep area. You must provide a well lit working environment – it's a health and safety issue. You simply cannot have people slicing up cucumber at speed in a dimly lit place. Spotlights are best.

One word of advice: replace dud bulbs as soon as possible. Nothing looks worse than a chandelier with twelve bulbs, five of which are out.

Juicer/blender

With most pieces of equipment it is best to buy industrial quality goods, not domestic. However, in the case of juicers and blenders, if you go for the top-of-the-range domestic models, the quality is such that they can withstand a lot of wear. The other point is that the commercial models are much more expensive. You could probably buy four or five domestic ones for the price of a single good commercial model.

Obviously if you find that you are doing numerous fresh orange juices and smoothies and the equipment is breaking down under the strain then you will have to consider the industrial variety.

Bake-off oven

I have mentioned bake-off ovens in Chapter 5. I am in no doubt that they can be a real asset to a sandwich-coffee bar. They are easy to use, provide scope for introducing new lines such as savoury snacks (individual quiches, pizzas, pasties and so on) and you can now lease them on very easy terms.

Walkie-talkies

If there is any significant separation between the serving area and the food prep area then there is an argument for walkie-talkie head-sets. This would be particularly so if the food prep area happened to be on the floor below. There's no doubt some people would think they looked pretty cool. And yelling at the top of your voice to the person in the back isn't likely to enhance the image of competent professionalism you want to create.

Fly-killer

These are small electrical wall units with the glacial light blue tubes. They have trays to catch all the corpses of various species which should be cleared out on a regular basis. A fly-killer should be positioned not too close to a door since wind renders it less effective. In addition it should not be placed near food preparation areas for obvious reasons.

Practical points for all equipment

- Keep all guarantees and manuals together in one place. If you have an office area in your house this would be best – things just seem to go missing in the shop.
- When it comes to buying equipment – get good quality things but don't get carried away and end up buying things you really don't need. With the more marginal items, start trading and see if you really need them.

Before we started I decided that I wanted to sell good quality hot chocolate. The man who was supplying a lot of our equipment showed me a brochure for a particular hot chocolate-making machine. He assured me the results would be excellent. The cost? In 1995, a mere £800! The incredible part is that we really did seriously consider buying it.

◆ Equipment is expensive. At the outset you seem to have a lot of money because you've got a loan from the bank. However, having to buy a new piece of equipment after a year's trading can be a real pain. *So look after what you've got.* You should, of course, maintain equipment in accordance with the manufacturer's instructions.

Apart from this, the single most important thing is to make sure that your staff know how to operate all the equipment properly. This means that you have to make sure you understand how to operate things properly yourself. This is particularly important when you get a new piece of equipment or take on a new member of staff.

> **Catering equipment has very little second-hand value. Buy good quality equipment, use it to the full and look after it. It makes financial sense.**

Furniture and fittings

Tables, chairs and stools

Assuming you have a bar along one or more walls then you will need stools. It may seem like an obvious point but before you install the bar make sure you can get stools which match it heightwise.

So far as choosing tables and chairs is concerned it really depends on the image you want to present. You might like the idea of a Bohemian-style café/seating area with an artistic or original image. If so, you will be well advised to go to a second-hand furniture shop or your nearest auctions and pick up a selection of old pieces of furniture there. They might be a bit of a hotch-potch but they will exude character and individuality.

However, don't forget your responsibility to the public. If you buy old furniture check that it is fit for its intended purpose, i.e. sturdy with no sticking out nails or screws. If a customer catches her expensive dress on a nail you won't be flavour of the month.

The other problem is that if you need to replace a couple of chairs you will find it harder to get good matches.

If you decide to buy new there is a large range of furniture available which is aimed at the catering industry generally: pubs, clubs, hotels, sandwich bars, cafés, etc. The obvious advantage is that they are specifically built for hard use, and if you need to replace them you can do so with identical pieces.

One other tip: try to find room for a (wonderfully named) poser's table. This is a free-standing weighted pole with one or two circular surfaces – absolutely ideal for putting in a window or small area of dead space. It has always been a source of disappointment to me that we have never found a suitable space for one.

Floor coverings

When it comes to floor coverings you really are in the same boat as any of the major high street stores; you must get good quality commercial products. Anything other than this will look tatty in no time. You will have hundreds of people traipsing over your floor in foul weather and fair. To get some ideas for your shop take a wander down your high street and see what the big stores use.

> **One tip: get small plastic covers to put on the ends of stool and chair legs to protect your floor coverings. If you buy new furniture your supplier will probably be able to provide these to you for a minimal extra charge.**

Make sure that you have a non-slip, heavy duty floor covering for the food preparation area.

Air conditioning or extractor?

You might think that air conditioning is a bit over the top for a small independent operation. But you will be surprised by the amount heat generated by a few refrigerated units. For a large part of the year this is not a problem – indeed it's an advantage because it helps to warm the place up, especially in the morning. In summer, however, when you open up in the morning, you will be hit by the kind of blast of warm air you get when you step off a plane in Mallorca in July.

If you have no means of cooling the shop the staff will complain – with justification. Working in this kind of heat is not pleasant.

You can buy a fan or two but all they do is re-cycle the air already in the shop. Admittedly summer doesn't last all that long in Britain and before you know where you are the staff will be asking for a heater. But do you really want to put up with two or three months of excessive heat in the shop?

You can install an air-conditioning system. It's the most effective solution. But it's expensive and quite complicated since you need to have a means of piping air to the exterior of the building. Whether you can install a system or not really depends on the nature of your particular unit and you will need expert advice. You can also hire an air conditioning unit on a weekly basis. However, it is very expensive. We recently got a quote for our second shop (which is about 850 sq. ft [78m^2]) of £800 for a month.

The simplest method of getting rid of the heat generated by refrigerated units is to install an extractor in the front window. It sucks the warm air out leaving the shop pleasantly cool. It is not very cheap. We had one installed in our first shop – a small unit of about 300 sq. ft (28m²) which cost a little under £600 including VAT. It was miraculously effective. Not only that but you can reverse the extractor so that in winter it operates to keep the warm air in the shop. In addition, the shop is cooler so the fridges don't have to work so hard and this reduces your electricity bills.

> **For a moderately-sized unit I think this is the best solution.**
> **BUT – you *must* take professional advice. If you simply buy one and**
> **get an electrician to fit it you might get the wrong size for your shop and it**
> **will only be partially effective. Get a professional to tell you what you need,**
> **and then if it doesn't work effectively you have someone to complain to.**

Computers

Make sure you exploit your multi-talented PC to the full.

Consider the following (non-exhaustive by any means) list of uses.

Printing

You can print (in any quantity or colour you want) professional-looking:

◆ menus

◆ contracts of employment

◆ correspondence on your chosen style of headed paper

◆ staff handbooks

◆ notices advertising for staff or advising of holiday dates, etc

◆ headed paper and compliments slips

◆ notices advertising new sandwiches, etc.

◆ envelopes

◆ outside catering invoices

◆ pro-forma order forms for cash and carry, supermarket, various suppliers.

And don't forget that you store all of these things so that updating them is easy as pie. Equally, if you write letters you store them on the computer so you have far less need to keep lots of paper copies.

Bookkeeping

Using spreadsheets you can enter details of money in, money out and VAT. This information can then be analysed and printed off for use by your accountants when preparing your accounts at the end of the year. The information is all stored so, for instance, it is easy for you to check back on the previous year's figures.

It is also possible to have a connection between your till and your computer (which may well be in your house) enabling them to 'talk' to each other. This means that when you go home after work the information about the day's take is already stored in the computer ready for you to work on. The company which supplies your till can give you information on this.

VAT and PAYE

You will need to buy software programs to load into your computer to deal with VAT and PAYE. They are not expensive and they are easy to use. They do all the hard work of calculating the payments due. In the case of PAYE you subscribe to a service which regularly updates your software and provides a support package.

Copying

Buy a scanner, connect it to your computer and, hey presto, you have the ability, amongst other things, to copy documents. A scanner is not expensive (well under £100) and saves you buying a photocopier or, worse still, going to your local library to get your copying done.

Internet and e-mail

You can surf the net for ideas and information about sandwiches/coffee/equipment and so on from all over the world. You could set up your own website as part of an expansion programme. A lot of people now encourage customers to e-mail orders in the morning which can then be collected at lunchtime.

If you are not computer literate this might all seem a bit daunting. However, the good news is that you don't need to understand how computers work to be able to use them to the benefit of your business. Do you really understand how a telephone or a DVD player works?

There are lots of inexpensive computer courses advertised in the press. Go on one of these, but also get a book out of the library and go in for a bit of trial and error. Surprise yourself.

Of course if you have (or have access to) teenagers you should get them to explain it all to you – just ask them to speak slowly!

Obviously there are costs associated with computers, but they're all tax deductible and the advantages, financial and otherwise, for your business are simply incalculable.

CHAPTER EIGHT

Staff and Day-To-Day Issues

Employing staff

There are conventional ways of advertising for staff: advertising in local papers, going through job agencies or placing details in your local job centre. The trouble is they all use up time and money. Not only that but you will end up with lots of applicants most of whom don't fit your preferred profile.

Assuming you have chosen a reasonably busy location for your sandwich-coffee bar, here's the Miller's Six Step Programme for getting the right staff with minimum hassle and virtually no expense.

- Print three copies of a sign advertising the job, including the hours to be worked. Do this on your computer and make it look professional.
- Put one copy on prominent display inside the shop and the other two in the front window.
- Prepare a questionnaire (which can of course be stored in your computer) to hand out to people who come in enquiring about the job. The questions should seek to elicit the basic information which you regard as most important. I have included a copy of our own questionnaire. Applicants should be encouraged to fill in the form in the shop. This enables the existing staff to observe them and form a first impression. This impression should be noted on the questionnaire.
- At your leisure look through the forms. You will be surprised how much of a feel you can get for a person from a spontaneously filled in form. Select those who seem most suitable.
- Arrange interviews as soon as possible. People looking for this kind of work really need the money and will often take the first decent job offer they get.
- Be prepared to make an instant decision after interviewing applicants. Again this is because they will usually want to be earning money as soon as possible and the best people are invariably snapped up quickly.

Millers Sandwich Bar

Prospective employee – personal details

Name:.. Today's date:..............................

Age:.. Date of birth:............................

Address: ....

....

....

....

Telephone number: ....

Do you smoke?...

Are you vegetarian? ....

Do you have a work permit/visa? (If applicable)...

Any holidays booked? ....

When could you start? ....

Any health problems?..

For how long are you looking for employment? ....

Previous experience in sandwich bar/similar – please give details.

....

....

....

....

....

Is there anyone we can contact for a reference? (If possible please provide telephone number)

....

....

....

If we think you might be suitable we will contact you in the next few days. If not, we won't, but thank you nonetheless for taking the time to complete this form.

Sample questionnaire/application form

We have found this system to be virtually foolproof. It has the added advantage that prospective employees get the chance to look at us – so if they don't fancy working in our kind of place they'll just walk on by.   Occasionally there are times when not so many people are looking for work so the choice is limited. At other times we have taken someone on within a few hours of putting the signs up.

With regard to our questionnaire, a few comments:

Are you a vegetarian?

I've nothing against vegetarians but if they are going to find it difficult to handle meat, cut off fat or gristle and so on, then working in a (non-vegetarian) sandwich-coffee bar might present problems all round. Clearly this is something which should be raised at interview.

For how long are you looking for employment?

Prospective staff are notorious for saying what they think you want to hear. Whatever they say it's not a guarantee of anything but it is good to know what they have in mind. If the reply is three months or less you have to ask yourself whether it is worth training somebody for such a short time. Then again, if they're good and you need cover for the summer it might be worth it, and people's plans can change.

Is there anyone we can contact for a reference?

Prospective staff will often bring a written reference or testimonial to the interview with details of a contact name. Speaking to someone for whom the person has worked is potentially valuable and if possible you should do this. But do it by phone. Remember the time factor. Not everybody is able to provide the name of a referee. If you think they fit the bill don't be put off by this. Your assessment is the most important thing by far.

> One of the best people we have ever employed applied to work for us within hours of arriving from Australia. She had no references and her address was a backpackers' hostel which she had not yet checked into.

New staff

Don't drop a new employee in at the deep end. You have to take time to train them to do things your way and also train them in matters of food hygiene and health and safety (see Chapter Nine). There's no rocket science involved but working efficiently in a sandwich bar involves working around other people and carrying out a lot of simple functions quickly, often under pressure. Training is best achieved by having new staff work under close supervision for a few hours each day for, say, three days. During this time they should get the chance to observe and carry out all the main aspects of the job. They should not be expected to work at lunchtime initially.

Of course, you may be lucky and get someone who has a lot of experience, in which case the amount of time spent training them can be reduced. There are clear advantages in taking on people with catering experience or training. *However, don't disregard those who don't have any experience.* If people have enthusiasm, an outgoing personality and a genuine interest in food – based preferably on having been brought up in a house where there was a wide variety of good food properly cooked – then you might well find they will make very good employees indeed.

A word about sandwich-coffee bar staff

Working in a sandwich-coffee bar is not a career or a vocation. It is never particularly well paid. Whilst you are entitled to expect hard work and a degree of commitment from your staff, the fact is that many of them are probably only working for you before going to university or college or as a way of financing their travels. You must be realistic about this.

> When we started my wife became upset when people, who appeared to like working for us, would come in one day and give a week's notice. I think the mistake she made was to expect that staff would or should share her commitment to the project.

Treat your staff well, get on well with them, but don't be surprised or feel let down when they move on after six months or so.

You may find that the work will suit a more mature person quite well; perhaps someone returning to work after having children who is looking for long-term part-time work. Such people may be prepared to make a longer term commitment and become very valuable members of your little team.

Employment law

There have been a number of significant additions to the laws affecting employees since 1997. Many of these changes have had the greatest impact on small businesses.

Before starting out in business it is important to have a clear understanding of the responsibilities and liabilities you will be taking on to those people who work for you.

The first point to understand is that *the great majority of the new provisions affect all businesses regardless of size.* I remember I once had a conversation with the proprietor of a small sandwich bar who expressed the view that the rules on holiday pay did not apply to him because his business was so small and because the people who worked for him were all part-timers. *Wrong on both counts.*

With few exceptions, the size of the business is irrelevant. And there is now no distinction between part-time and full-time workers – both groups benefit from the new provisions.

The other important point is that over many years the emphasis has increasingly come to be on **fairness** and **transparency** when dealing with employees. It is a philosophy that makes sense. If people feel that their terms of employment are reasonable and clearly understood from the outset they will tend to be happier in their work – and more productive from the employer's point of view.

Let's consider some of the most important points which will affect you in more detail.

Minimum wage

You are legally obliged to pay your staff no less than the applicable minimum wage. The current rates are:

£3.57 per hour for all staff under the age of 18 who are no longer of compulsory school age (in general this means people of 16 and 17).

£4.83 per hour for staff aged 18 – 21 inclusive. This called the development rate.

£5.80 per hour for 22 years and above.
The National Minimum Wage helpline: 0800 9172368. www.hmrc.gov.uk/nmw/help.htm

Paid holiday

All staff are entitled to paid holiday up to a maximum of 5.6 weeks times their usual working week. There is no qualifying period. So for instance, if someone has worked for you for six months they will be entitled to 2.4 weeks times their usual working week in holiday pay when they head off to the sun. Bear in mind though that 'a week' equates to the length of week a particular employee works; part time staff are entitled to holiday pay on a *pro-rata* basis. The holiday entitlement is not additional to bank holidays – there is in fact no statutory right to take bank or similar holidays off. Surprisingly enough this even applies to Christmas Day!

An employee is not entitled as of right to take holidays on a particular date – but hopefully this will be a matter discussed and agreed well in advance. You on the other hand, are entitled to insist that holidays be taken at particular times. For instance, you may wish to close the shop in August to coincide with school holidays. This is your privilege and you are entitled to insist that staff holidays be taken at this time. Again, you should make this clear as early as possible, preferably at interview.

> **For more information you should visit the website www.direct.gov.uk and put "holiday pay" in the search box. You can also obtain information from your local Jobcentre.**

Contracts and written particulars of employment

A contract of employment exists as soon as an employee starts working for you, thus demonstrating that they accept the terms discussed when you offered them the job. However, in addition, employees who work for you for four weeks or more are entitled to receive a written statement of employment particulars *within two months of commencing work*. You may have particular matters you want to deal with in the statement, but the main terms to be included are:

- ◆ The names of the employer and employee
- ◆ The date when the employment (and the period of continuous employment) began
- ◆ Remuneration and the intervals at which it is to be paid
- ◆ Hours of work
- ◆ Holiday entitlement
- ◆ Entitlement to sick leave including any entitlement to sick pay
- ◆ The entitlement of employer and employee to notice of termination
- ◆ Job title or a brief job description
- ◆ Where it is not permanent, the period for which the employment is expected to continue or, if it is for a fixed term, the date when it is to end
- ◆ A note giving certain details of the employer's disciplinary and grievance procedures
- ◆ Any pensions or pension schemes.

> **If you don't want to write it all out yourself you can obtain an 'Example form of a written statement of employment particulars' (PL 700A) from your local Jobcentre which meets the requirements of the legislation. Once you've done the first one it can be stored in your computer for future use.**

Maternity and Paternity Leave

A female employee is entitled to a total period of up to 52 weeks' maternity leave regardless of her length of service – though she is not obliged to take all of the leave she is entitled to. The employee has to tell her employer about her pregnancy at least 15 weeks before the beginning of the week the baby is due. Maternity leave can start any time from the eleventh week before the expected date of confinement up to the birth itself. Once you have been notified that an employee wishes to take maternity leave you should write to her within 28 days telling her the date when the maternity leave will end. At the end of the period of maternity leave the employee is entitled to return to her original job if she chose to restrict her period of leave to 26 weeks (ordinary maternity leave). Even if she takes longer than 26 weeks she is entitled to her old job back unless you can demonstrate that this would not be possible or practical. Clearly this might create real problems for the small business.

An employee is entitled to Statutory Maternity Pay (SMP) for up to 39 weeks if she has been employed by the same employer continuously for at least 26 weeks into the 15th week before the baby is due and has been earning an average of £95 a week (before tax). SMP is payable at the rate of 90 per cent of an employee's average weekly earnings for the first six weeks and then up to £123.06 for the remaining 33 weeks. Tax and National Insurance are paid by the employee in the usual way, as on regular wages. You then reclaim the majority of SMP from the employee's National Insurance contributions and other payments.

Paternity leave is available to fathers who have been employed for at least 26 weeks by the end of the 15th week before the start of the week when the baby is due and who are earning on average £95 per week. If earning less than this they will be entitled to some unpaid paternity leave. Such fathers will require to be fully involved in the child's upbringing; the purpose of paternity leave is to allow fathers to support the mother and care for the baby. The entitlement is to one or two weeks – to be taken all at once, not odd days here and there. It cannot be taken before the baby is born and must be completed no later than 56 days after the baby is born. The rate of Statutory Paternity Pay is the same as that for SMP.

Adoptive parents also have certain rights to paid leave.

These are fairly complex matters which will probably only occur rarely. For more detailed information you should visit the website www.direct.gov.uk and search for the relevant items. You can also obtain information from your local Jobcentre. I recommend that if such situations ever do arise that you discuss the position with your employee openly and frankly as soon as possible.

Statutory sick pay

If a member of staff is off sick for four or more days you will become liable for statutory sick pay. The current rate is £79.15 per week for employees between 16 and 65 years whose earnings exceed £95 per week. You are not required to pay SSP for the first three days off. The payment of SSP continues for a maximum of 28 weeks after which time the employee can make a claim for employment support allowance from the DSS. Within seven days of the first day of sickness the employee should complete a self-certification form regarding his or her situation. The form, SC2, is downloadable from the internet. You can also require the employee to provide a medical certificate if you wish.

You can recover some of the statutory sick pay (SSP) you have paid out if you qualify under the **Percentage Threshold Scheme (PTS)**. The general principle of the PTS is that if in a tax month the total SSP you pay to all of your employees is more than 13 per cent of your total gross employer's plus employees' Class 1 National Insurance contributions (NICs) for the same tax month, you are entitled to a refund of the excess. You can recover the amount of SSP you are entitled to by taking it from your NICs and PAYE (Pay As You Earn) payments. If the amount of SSP you are entitled to recover is more than your monthly NICs and PAYE payments, you can deduct the balance from your next month's payment.

Once more these matters are fairly complex and you can obtain more information from the relevant section of the HMRC website: www.hmrc.gov.uk or phone the helpline: 0845 143 143

Stakeholder pensions

If you employ five or more people then you may be required to set up a stakeholder pension scheme to which your employees can contribute if they wish. This is an area for which specialist advice will be required. You should visit the website of the Department for Works and Pensions: www.dwp.gov.uk or contact the British Sandwich Association (details at the end of the book). Your insurance broker may also be able to help.

Enquiries should be addressed to the British Sandwich Association, Association House, 18c Moor Street, Chepstow. NP16 5DB Tel: 01291 636333. Website: www.sandwich.org.uk

Dismissal of staff

If you dismiss someone you have employed *for a continuous period of one year or more* they have the right to make a claim against you at an industrial tribunal if they think the dismissal was unfair. If you do find yourself in the situation of wanting to dismiss someone you must act fairly. The law recognises five areas which can give rise to fair dismissal:

◆ A reason related to the employee's capability or qualification for the job
◆ A reason related to the employee's conduct
◆ Redundancy – broadly this is where the employer's need for employees to do certain work has ceased or diminished or is expected to do so
◆ A statutory restriction preventing continuation of the employment
◆ Some other substantial reason which could justify dismissal.

At all times the question will be whether you treated the employee reasonably in the circumstances. Don't act without warning. Tell people what they are doing wrong and give them a chance to improve. If problems persist then it is important to give written warnings before finally deciding to dismiss someone. It is regarded as desirable that employees who are at risk of being dismissed are able to meet with their employer to discuss the situation in the company of a representative – a friend or adviser.

Anyone who has ever run a small business will tell you how difficult such strictures can be. The chances are you work at very close quarters with two or three staff in one shop. Written warnings and grievance procedures – perfectly feasible in large multi-layered organisations – will be largely impractical. However, if you do run into problems the question you have to ask yourself as you try to deal with the situation is: *if the employee makes a claim against me, what will an industrial tribunal make of the way I handled it?*

These situations are mercifully rare. The main thing is to get the right staff in the first place.

The other extremely important thing is to respond quickly if you experience problems with staff. Don't let problems fester. This is particularly relevant in the days after you take someone new on. You generally know quite quickly whether a new employee is going to work out. If, after a week or so, you are pretty sure that they are not suitable it's far better to terminate their employment right away. Don't put up with things because you you can't face telling someone they're not right for the job. If you do, you are just storing up problems for the future.

**Make it easier on yourself by always making it clear at interview
that there will be a trial period of, say, two weeks.**

If you do decide to dismiss an employee you must give certain minimum periods of notice. These vary according to the length of time the employee has worked for you:

◆ between four weeks and two years: one week

◆ two years: two weeks

◆ for each extra year: add an extra week up to a maximum of twelve weeks.

If someone is guilty of gross misconduct then you can dismiss them on the spot. This applies to being caught stealing for instance, though you are still supposed to listen to their side of the story before taking action.

If you take someone on and it doesn't work out and they have worked for you for less than four weeks you should give them reasonable notice. This could be a day or two or possibly just the rest of the afternoon. In such situations the employee concerned might well not want to hang around.

In general, dismissal is a matter you should consider seriously. The upper limit for awards at industrial tribunals has increased dramatically in recent times and is currently £65,300, though such awards are highly exceptional.

For employees the requirements are less onerous. An employee has to give at least one week's notice if employed continuously for a month or more, but this period is unaffected by length of service.

The one year qualifying period for unfair dismissal claims does not apply in the cases where dismissal takes place on grounds related to:

◆ sex

◆ race

◆ disability

◆ a complaint about a breach of an employee's statutory rights

In these cases there is no qualifying period at all.

**For further information visit the relevant section of the website www.direct.gov.uk
which contains a wealth of information and links to other relevant sites. Your local
Jobcentre will also be able to provide information.**

Employment rights on the transfer of undertakings

In other words, what happens when you take over a going concern which employs one or more members of staff. The relevant regulations apply specifically 'where all or part of a sole trader's business or partnership is sold or otherwise transferred'. The new employer takes over the contracts of employment of all employees who were employed immediately before the transfer 'or who would have been if they had not been unfairly dismissed for a reason connected with the transfer'. These words are taken from a legal judgement on this issue. The effect is that an employer cannot just pick and choose which employees to take on.

It follows that when a business is sold, staff cannot be dismissed simply because of the sale unless there is some justification. This could be 'economic, technical or organisational'. So for instance, if the previous business employed three people but you are sure you only need two then you may be able to dismiss one, but you would need to be able to justify this – perhaps because you intend to spend more time in the shop than the previous owner.

The staff you inherit have exactly the same rights with you as they did with the previous owner of the business. If there is a fundamental change for the worse in their conditions this could well give them the right to terminate their employment and make a claim for unfair 'constructive' dismissal. Even if the dismissal of staff is regarded as reasonable they may be entitled to a redundancy payment.

As you can see, taking over a going concern is not without its problems.

For more detailed information you should consult the relevant section of the website www.direct.gov.uk or visit your local Jobcentre.

There are countless laws and regulations on the subject of employees' rights. You can't possibly be expected to know them all. There is one particularly useful government booklet which contains a lot of information on a wide variety of areas. It is called 'Individual Rights of Employees' (PL 716 Rev 8). It is available via the website of the Department for Business Enterprise & Regulatory Reform (www.berr.gov.uk)

Remember also that if you become a member of the **Federation of Small Businesses** they have solicitors on call who can also give you up-to-date information – though rather than have a general chat about the state of current employment law their brief is to deal with specific queries about problems you encounter. A valuable service. Every local FSB branch arranges regular talks on current issues affecting small businesses, and you get the chance to question experts about your particular concerns. There is also a regular magazine which contains articles on small business matters – often before they are widely known. Forewarned is forearmed.

> **The address of the Federation of Small Businesses' head office is Sir Frank Whittle Way, Blackpool Business Park, Blackpool FY4 2FE. Tel: 01253 348046. They have a helpline: 01235 336 000. Website: www.fsb.org.uk**

General inquiries will also be dealt with by either your local Jobcentre or ACAS (Advisory, Conciliation and Arbitration Service) – see your local phone book for details.

> **When it comes to employees' rights there are lots of sources of assistance. Don't hesitate to make use of them if there are things you are not sure about.**

Up to this point I've talked about legal matters. I now want to discuss two points which you won't find in any Act of Parliament but which I believe are highly relevant to the successful running of a sandwich-coffee bar: the staff handbook and staff meetings.

Staff handbook

I can hear the groans already: 'I want to sell sandwiches and coffee, not a write a book'. This would have been my view too before we opened our first shop – but not now.

When you plan your business you build up in your mind a vision of how you want it to be. You make lots of assumptions about numerous things. When you interview a prospective employee you will get over some of this vision – but only some. When, a week after they start, you arrive at the shop to find them standing outside the shop smoking a cigarette you are annoyed and flustered. 'We don't do that sort of thing here' you think and perhaps say. But did you make this absolutely clear at interview? No, you forgot that particular point. So you have to make it clear now, when the employee has spent a week thinking something else – so they are not greatly pleased either.

A staff handbook should contain your vision and your particular policies on a wide range of issues. It is also a great opportunity to spell out in detail the importance of particular matters ranging from personal hygiene to what to do if there is an accident – which are legal requirements. In other words, it can also help you to ensure that as far as possible your employees comply with relevant laws. See pages 193-7 for an extract from our staff handbook.

A staff handbook should be given to someone when you take them on. Ideally they should have a day or two in which to read it before starting work. Make sure you ask them if they have read it when they come to work on the first day and give them the opportunity to ask questions or seek clarification about any points.

A staff handbook can be quite light-hearted at times, more businesslike at others. There really are no hard and fast rules – you should include those things that are important to you.

> **And remember: when you've done it once you can store it in your computer ready to be printed off when you next take somebody on.**

So what are the kinds of things which you should consider including in your staff handbook? The things which you regard as important for delivering your vision and also the efficient day-to-day running of the shop. Many things will have been explained during the interview and initial training but the handbook acts as a good aide-memoire throughout a person's period of employment with you.

- **Specific duties:** it is important that people understand what it is they are expected to do. You won't have time to spell out every last thing at interview.
- **Dress code and personal hygiene:** to include such things as not wearing strong smelling perfume or bracelets, washing hands regularly and having long hair properly tied back at all times.
- **Time-keeping:** so important – you really need to get going first thing in the morning. Lateness by one member of staff puts extra pressure on the others. We tell people to arrive five minutes before their start time so that they are actually ready to start work at 8.00 not ready to start getting ready for work.
- **Dealing with customers:** always being polite and attentive. What to do if someone is dissatisfied with something. What to do if a customer is drunk or offensive. Fortunately these things are very rare but staff, particularly younger staff, should be given some guidance on such matters.
- **Smoking:** now prohibited by law anywhere inside the premises. A more difficult issue is staff wanting to smoke outside the front of the shop. I regard this as unacceptable. It creates a bad image and inevitably the smell of tobacco accompanies people back into the shop. So how are you going to deal with it? It's up to you!
- **Moodiness:** this is a really difficult one. We all of us have days when we have a lot on our minds, when we really don't feel much like being outgoing. You have to accept that

staff will on occasion be a little under par. However, some people go beyond this – and you cannot afford to put up with it in a small sandwich-coffee bar. *A bad atmosphere is created which affects staff and customers alike.*

> We once had an employee who could be pleasant and chatty and then come in the next day miserable and withdrawn; questions would be met with monosyllabic replies. It was hell. The trouble was she was well able to do the job. Frankly the situation would have been much easier to deal with if she hadn't been. Eventually we did dismiss her. She was completely taken aback. I wrote to her explaining the difficulties she caused. I hope she learned something from the experience. I would not have liked to have defended that one in an industrial tribunal.

◆ **Procedure following an accident:** who to notify, whether it might in some circumstances be appropriate to close the shop.
◆ **Cheques:** the correct procedure to be followed if somebody pays by cheque.
◆ **Dogs:** with the exception of guide dogs you should not allow dogs in the shop. Apart from the obvious breach of hygiene a badly behaved dog could make a considerable nuisance of itself in a busy lunchtime queue.
◆ **Music/tv/radio:** the real question here is who are these things for? Many owners of businesses would say the customers, but a lot of people working in shops would say the staff. It really is your choice but my view is that there is a balance to be struck which aims to please (which is different from not to offend) everybody. However, I am in no doubt that what is paramount is the atmosphere which is created in the shop.

> Imagine this: you allow the staff to choose the kind of music which is played. Let's say you have a fairly high turnover of staff – not uncommon with sandwich bars. This means that a regular customer might get The Beatles one week, Eminem the next and Miles Davis the one after that.
>
> I think this is a bad idea. I believe that the boss has to exercise editorial control over the musical output – to ensure that whatever music is played fits in with their vision. What you are selling to the customer is not just a good sandwich but also an image and an ambience. And no matter how good the music, the volume should always be at an appropriate level.

If you do play recorded music in the shop (and you'll be pretty unusual if you don't) you'll need two licences. These should be obtained, along with further information, from: PPL (formerly Phonographic Performance Ltd), 1 Upper James Street, London W1F 9DE Tel: 020 7534 1000. Fax: 020 7534 1111. www.ppluk.com

The PPL represents the interests of recording companies who assign their copyright to the PPL. For a unit of 500 square metres the current annual cost is about £100.

You also need a licence from another organisation which deals specifically with the interests of the artists. (If you *only* play a radio then you will only need this second licence.) The Performing Rights Society, 29–33 Berners Street, London W1T 3AB
Tel: 020 7580 5544. Licensing hotline: 0800 0684828. www.prs.co.uk

The cost of the PRS licence will be similar to that for PPL.

If you intend to have a TV in the shop or indeed a TV-enabled computer (a PC with a broadcast card) or TV receiving equipment which is capable of receiving TV programmes you will need a TV licence. One licence covers any number of sets on one site. You do not need a licence if a TV set cannot receive programmes and is only used for closed circuit monitoring, or for showing pre-recorded videos or as a monitor for a computer.

◆ **Procedure for making a sandwich to order:** all the questions to ask in the correct order (type of bread, butter/margarine/salt/pepper, etc).
◆ **Portion control:** large sandwich manufacturing factories can churn out thousands of identical portion controlled sandwiches every day. With small independents it's not an exact science. The aim should be to arrive at a balance which is fair to the customer and fair to the business. Make clear the way you want it done during initial training.
◆ **Procedures for particular kinds of food:**
  - cutting fat off smoked turkey
  - not cutting open avocados which aren't ready
  - an indication of the quantities which should go into each sandwich
  - defrosting prawns.

> **The possibilities are endless. It is your opportunity to put down in black and white the way you want things done – and get this over to your staff. It's a good idea for a business of any size. The process of writing things down also helps you to clarify your own thoughts on all the important issues you will be responsible for.**

Staff meetings

In a small shop unit you might say there are numerous opportunities for discussion about anything and everything. This is true up to a point. However, you are likely to be interrupted all the time. If it is a matter of a personal nature or any degree of controversy, then discussing it during working hours with customers around is not appropriate.

Staff meetings are particularly desirable if you have new staff. You've given them a staff handbook and they've done their initial period of training but inevitably questions will arise – or it will be obvious that they are doing some things wrongly. A brief meeting held after the shop has closed provides the appropriate forum to discuss such matters.

Such meetings are good for experienced staff too. They provide an opportunity to discuss matters beyond the basics: why things are going well, why they're not, new customer preferences and so on. This can provide very valuable feedback from the people who work at the coalface.

They also give staff the opportunity to raise matters of concern to them. In such situations try to make it as easy as possible for people to talk freely; there is absolutely nothing to be gained from having some source of irritation or frustration festering below the surface.

It is not necessary to have meetings at set intervals. You could end up looking for things to say. I think it is for you as director of the show to sense when a meeting would be a good idea. Staff should be made aware in the handbook that you have staff meetings from time to time and that they can request one if they have an issue they wish to discuss.

Employing a manager

For a small independent operation starting up, it would be surprising if the initial turnover could justify the cost of a manager. Further, such a person might have different ideas from you and immediately there could be conflict. It would, of course, be appealing to have somebody else take the strain in the shop thus freeing you up to attend to many other jobs such as going to the cash and carry, book-keeping or making soup. However, at the outset it is best for you to be involved hands-on in the shop most of the time. It means that you are there to make spot decisions and iron out problems.

If you do decide to have a manager later on the best way to achieve this is by internal promotion. You know them, they know you – and how you want things done.

I have known a couple of sandwich bar owners who have taken people on as managers (not by internal promotion) to reduce their workload and also to try to increase turnover. What happened was that their wage bill went up a lot but their turnover stayed about the same.

You really have to ask yourself if you need a manager. Assuming you are in the shop a lot and that you are taking responsibility for all important decisions, are you sure you want to pay somebody extra for taking on a few extra responsibilities? The important questions are:

◆ will it improve the quality of your life?
◆ will you still make enough money for yourself?

If the answer to both questions is in the affirmative then it may well work for you, but internal promotion will invariably be best.

If you decide to expand your empire by opening a second outlet then, of course, the arguments in favour of having a manager in one of the shops will become much more powerful. This subject is further explored in Chapter Eleven.

Banking and money matters

The float
One extra expense right at the start is the float. £100 will probably be sufficient. Obviously you should have a reasonable selection of notes and coins. Some people take out the next day's float at the end of the day and leave it in the shop. Personally I prefer not to leave money in the shop overnight. It's your choice, but if you do leave money overnight check with your insurance company or insurance brokers that it is covered. Always remember to leave the till open. Insurance companies will almost certainly not pay for damage to tills left closed overnight.

Paying by credit/debit card
Should you offer your customers the possibility of paying by credit or debit card? I do think it encourages people to spend more, in which case it is potentially good for business. However, you will be charged approximately 2–3% of each transaction for this service. I'm not in any doubt that sooner or later payment by plastic card will become the norm. Equally, given the size of most transactions, I think sandwich-coffee bars will be amongst the last to succumb.

Paying by cheque

If people pay by cheque it is vital that staff know the correct procedure for checking bank cards and noting relevant details. You should also consider charging an extra 25p or so per transaction to reflect the bank charge you will incur for processing the cheque.

Luncheon vouchers

What about Luncheon Vouchers? Again the charge to you is about 2% and again there is a certain amount of paperwork and administration. You post the Luncheon Vouchers to an organisation called Accor Services who then post a cheque to you eight working days after they receive the vouchers. For a charge of 5% they will reduce the eight day period to one day. For more information contact new sales enquiries – 0845 3651217.

Banking the takings

You will probably want to bank the takings two or three times a week. You might be taken aback at what banks charge for handling lots of cash. One way round this is to pay the bulk of the cash into a building society (or one of the banks which were formerly building societies) and then have them write a cheque in favour of your bank. It's quite a lot of messing around but the saving amounts to many hundreds of pounds a year – and you soon get into a system.

You can pay bills in cash and cut out the bank altogether. However, the cash departments of some of your suppliers will be many miles from your shop so that posting cheques is the obvious method of payment. Far simpler nowadays is internet banking which allows you to pay bills at the click of a mouse.

Security

There are two situations where security – of you and your staff – must be considered:

1. when cashing up at the end of the day. Any reasonably smart criminal will realise that this process happens at about the same time every day. It is therefore important that before cashing up begins the shop should be locked.
2. when going to the bank to get change. In this situation a member of staff will be walking along the road carrying quite a lot of cash. Make sure that this outing takes place at different times of day and that the money is in a nondescript polythene bag or something similar which will not attract the wrong kind of attention.

CHAPTER NINE

Food Hygiene and Health and Safety

Food hygiene

To say this is a subject which is taken more seriously than it used to be is something of an understatement. Even people with no particular interest in food will be only too familiar with BSE ('mad cow disease'), E Coli, salmonella and listeria. The last few years have been traumatic for the food and catering industries.

One of the consequences has been that rules and regulations on food hygiene are now enforced more strictly than in the past. This became particularly apparent in the late nineties. Sandwich-coffee bars and other food outlets suddenly started receiving more visits from environmental health officers on a mission. It was clear that they were under orders to be far more proactive in getting people to observe the rules. This remains the position. Anyone wanting to open any kind of food outlet must realise that food hygiene is a matter of prime importance.

> **Whilst it may be true that the places of most concern to the authorities are large food processors, butchers' shops and the like, be in no doubt that sandwich-coffee bars are also regarded as high risk – and new operations will come under particularly close scrutiny.**

Want some more good news? The people who police the laws, the environmental health officers (EHOs) generally arrive in your premises unannounced and will want to ask lots of questions and look at all aspects of your operation. This can be quite traumatic for younger or newer members of staff who have to deal with this if you're not there. They might have forgotten the correct temperature for storing cooked meats and feel quite flustered. Even the experts will tell you that the law on food hygiene is complex and ever changing, **but** ignorance of the law will be no excuse in the event that you are found to be doing something wrong!

There is some good news as well.

◆ A great deal of what is contained in the various laws, rules and regulations boils down to common sense.

◆ Environmental health officers are reasonable people. Whilst they do have the power to take enforcement action and even close shops down in extreme cases, their aim is to be constructive in helping you to run your particular business successfully whilst complying with the relevant laws.

◆ EHOs must comply with statutory codes and guidelines when it comes to enforcing the law. They are not entitled to push people around and if they do you will have recourse against them.

◆ EHOs assess the likely risk associated with particular food outlets. So long as you are seen to be making reasonable efforts to follow the advice and directions of your local EHO you will find that you will be regarded as low risk – you will receive fewer visits, leaving officers more time to concentrate on the problem places.

Whilst there are numerous laws on the subject of food hygiene, the main aim of all of them is the rather noble one of protecting human health. Of great relevance to sandwich-coffee bars are the Food Safety (General Food Hygiene) Regulations 1995 and the Food Safety (Temperature Control) Regulations 1995. These apply to England and Wales and Scotland. There are equivalent regulations for Northern Ireland.

There is one particular publication which deals with the subject of compliance with these regulations. It is called *Industry Guide To Good Hygiene Practice: Catering Guide*. The guide is a government inspired document painstakingly prepared by leading experts in the field. It is published by Chadwick House Group Ltd. It currently costs £3.60.

Whatever other publications you consider buying I recommend that you get hold of a copy of this guide well before you sell your first sandwich. If you don't have any catering training it will open your eyes to the various issues you will have to address when setting up and operating your business. It also gives details of other publications which deal in greater detail with specific subjects.

What's more, it is particularly useful and relevant because enforcement officers must give due consideration to it when assessing compliance in particular cases. You will, so to speak, be singing from the same hymn sheet.

Areas of concern

Here are the main health and hygiene areas of concern to sandwich-coffee bars which are dealt with in the guide:

1. Identification of steps critical to food safety

The obligation here is to identify possible food hazards in your particular business. The jargon is 'Hazard Analysis Critical Control Point' (HACCP). A food hazard basically means any kind of contamination which could cause harm to the consumer – i.e. your beloved customers. The three areas are:

◆ Bacteria or other micro-organisms that cause food poisoning
◆ Chemicals – cleaning materials or pest baits for example
◆ Foreign material such as bits of glass.

Your job is to analyse and identify the possible areas of the shop or stages of production which could be hazardous and take appropriate steps to eradicate the risks. This could mean ensuring good personal hygiene practices by your staff or cleaning and disinfection of equipment or repair of a faulty piece of electrical equipment. Having identified potential hazards it is not enough to simply deal with them once, you have to be able to demonstrate that you have taken steps to introduce systems to deal with the hazards and monitor these systems for continuing effectiveness.

2. Food hygiene supervision and instruction and/or training

The exact wording of the regulation is:

'The proprietor of a food business shall ensure that food handlers engaged in the food business are supervised and /or trained in food hygiene matters commensurate with their activities.'

In larger organisations there may be job demarcation in which case different types and levels of supervision and training may be required. However, in most small independent sandwich-coffee bars everybody does everything so all staff – and you – are in the same boat.

When you take on new staff you should instruct them in the **essentials of food hygiene** before they start work. These are fairly obvious and include:

◆ personal hygiene and clean clothing
◆ washing hands thoroughly before handling food, after using the toilet, after breaks and so on
◆ reporting any skin, nose, throat, stomach or bowel troubles or infected wounds
◆ clean-as-you-go – keep all equipment and surfaces clean and free from debris as far as possible.

All staff should also receive **hygiene awareness instruction**, ideally within four weeks of starting work. This includes such items as:

◆ cross-contamination – causes and ways of prevention
◆ awareness of pests
◆ food storage – the protection of different foods and the maintenance of correct temperatures
◆ waste disposal, acceptable cleaning and disinfection practices.

> I recommend that you include those which you consider important for your business in your staff handbook as bullet points under the general heading of food hygiene.

The other matter which is now taken very seriously indeed is **formal training**. There are three levels of training: basic/elementary (Level 1), intermediate (Level 2) and advanced (Level 3). Levels 2 and 3 are appropriate for those who intend to make a career in catering and who progress to jobs such as managers or supervisors who handle any types of food.

> Everybody (unless they never handle any unwrapped food) should be trained to elementary level within three months of starting work.

Larger organisations sometimes arrange for in-house training. However, small businesses generally send their staff on professionally run day-long courses. Such courses usually last about six hours. The aim is to teach the basic principles of food hygiene. The courses will cover:

◆ food poisoning and its sources
◆ simple (very simple, honest) microbiology
◆ premises and equipment
◆ common food hazards
◆ personal hygiene
◆ preventing food contamination
◆ food poisoning – symptoms and causes
◆ cleaning and disinfection
◆ legal obligations
◆ pest control
◆ effective temperature control of food.

Courses are run by various organisations including:

◆ The Chartered Institute of Environmental Health
◆ The Royal Institute of Public Health and Hygiene
◆ The Royal Society of Health
◆ The Royal Environmental Health Institute of Scotland
◆ Society of Food Hygiene Technology.

In addition your local EHO will be able to give you details of suitable courses in your area.

A one-day course lasting six hours doesn't sound too onerous but this can create problems. You may well have a reasonably high turnover of staff. So this means you might be having to send somebody on one of these courses every few months or so. That's one day every few months or so when you don't have the services of one member of staff (in a small place possibly one third of the workforce), who will nonetheless expect to be paid and receive travelling expenses. And there's the cost of the course itself – probably £75 plus VAT minimum. Of course it's all tax deductible but you have to pay for it upfront.

There is one way round this which you might want to consider.

If you undergo and pass the advanced course you can apply to be registered with your local authority as a food hygiene trainer. This means that you are then regarded as sufficiently qualified to teach your own staff what they need to know to satisfy the requirements of the regulations.

Not only that but you could then have a sideline of teaching the course to other people. You could use your own premises for this, possibly at weekends or evenings or you could go to students' places of work. This could be a useful source of extra revenue, though your local environmental health department may require you to undergo some further training with them before allowing you to teach the general public – check with them.

But of course, as always, nothing is ever simple or easy.

◆ The course lasts approximately 30 hours and is usually spread over ten weeks (although there are shorter intensive courses available as well).
◆ It involves a fair amount of academic work including essay writing and there's an all-day exam at the end which includes an oral test.

♦ It's expensive, anything between £600 and £1,000, but it will pay for itself eventually. It's all tax deductible and it will provide you with a marketable skill.

With the increasing levels of employment in the hospitality and catering industries and the increased emphasis on training you might well find that prospective employees already have a qualification. I think that is the government's aim. This will then be a factor in deciding whether to take somebody on. *But don't employ somebody who doesn't seem quite right just for the sake of saving £100 or so.*

3. The rules of hygiene

This area is concerned with the premises and those parts of the premises in which food or drink is prepared, served or stored. It includes ancillary areas such as toilets, staff rooms, cellars and so on.

The list of requirements covered under this heading is long and detailed. It includes:

♦ Maintenance of the premises in good repair and condition.
♦ Suitable layout, design and construction to permit adequate cleaning and disinfection.
♦ Regular cleaning of all areas of premises – it is recommended that you keep a record of this. Pro-forma cleaning schedules can easily be produced on a PC.
♦ Sufficient space in food preparation and storage areas to allow preparation of high risk foods on separate work surfaces.
♦ An adequate number of suitably located wash basins with hot and cold water.
♦ Provision of suitable and sufficient natural or mechanical ventilation – this avoids the build-up of heat or humidity levels which might endanger the safety of the food.
♦ Sanitary conveniences to be fitted with adequate natural or mechanical ventilation.
♦ In rooms where food is prepared floor and wall surfaces must be maintained in sound condition and must be easy to clean.
♦ Equipment used for the preparation of food must be kept clean and maintained in good enough condition as to minimise the risk of contamination of the food.
♦ Food waste must be stored in suitable containers which should be emptied and cleaned regularly.
♦ Routine checks should be made on deliveries of food to check that they are in good condition and not contaminated – this provision is more relevant to items such as raw meat.

◆ Raw food material must be properly stored in such a way as to preserve it in the best possible condition and avoid contamination.

◆ Where appropriate, adequate provision must be made for any necessary washing of food – in practice this means that separate sinks must be provided for food preparation and equipment if the volume of preparation demands it.

◆ Vehicles used for the transport of food (quite possibly your private car) must be kept clean and in good condition and there must be adequate provision for the separation of food items from other things being transported in the vehicle.

◆ Adequate measures must be in place to ensure pests are controlled. Apart from an electric fly-killer you should, at the first sign of bugs or mice droppings, call in a pest control expert and enter into an annual contract whereby they will treat the problem, put down bait or traps and attend immediately if there is any recurrence. The contractor will keep a record of treatments which is evidence that you are complying with this particular requirement. This can then be shown to an EHO during a spot check. It may well be sensible to enter into such a contract before any problems arise.

◆ Domestic premises: the provisions are essentially the same as for the shop. (See also Chapter Six for points specific to domestic premises.)

If you take over a going concern you will have to give consideration to the current state of the unit. If it all looks pretty run down you may well find that the cost of bringing it up to acceptable standards is considerable. I'm not saying this should put you off – but you must factor this into your overall start-up costs.

I mentioned previously the value of consulting an EHO early. Their advice on this area will be particularly useful and should be sought before you commit yourself to anything. You might well find that the EHO knows all about the premises in question from previous dealings!

Temperature controls

This is a particularly important area since foods stored at too high a temperature provide fertile sites for the growth of undesirable bacteria. *Industry Guide to Good Hygiene Practice* referred to previously contains details of the different kinds of foods and the rules and temperatures which apply to them. It also explains the different methods of testing the temperatures of food as well as refrigerated units.

Leaving aside any legal requirements, it is a very good idea to test the temperature of refrigerated units on a daily basis. If a unit fails the temperature only rises slowly. Staff might not be aware of the problem for some time. Getting early warning of problems is much better than suddenly discovering at four o'clock in the afternoon that your fridge has broken down and you have a lot of food which is about to go off.

It is regarded as good practice to keep written records of temperature checks. You can produce suitable simple pro forma charts on a PC. In the event of any concern on the part of an EHO the production of temperature charts will help you to demonstrate that you have exercised 'due diligence' in storing food – a key test in such situations.

From the point of view of a sandwich-coffee bar proprietor it is interesting, and to me not a little surprising, that cold food may be kept at levels above the usual limits (which are up to 5°C for *refrigerated equipment* and 8°C for the *actual food*) for up to four hours 'for certain practicalities'. What this means is that if you make up some sandwiches at 10 o'clock in the morning you can display them on an unrefrigerated shelf at ambient temperatures until two o'clock.

Of course in the event of any complaint by an EHO the onus is on you to demonstrate that the food in question was all right at the relevant time.

My view is that this provision is a recipe for substandard sandwiches being sold to the public. Sandwiches made from fresh bread and ingredients are designed to be eaten at the earliest opportunity. Not only that but whilst they are being offered for sale, perhaps on a warm summer's day, they should be kept in the best possible condition from the customer's point of view. To me this means displaying them only on a refrigerated shelf.

I suspect this provision is a sop to take-aways set up years ago, before the days when food hygiene was such a hot issue. In my view anybody starting a sandwich bar now would be committing commercial suicide by selling unrefrigerated sandwiches. The public are used to and expect better. A great deal of helpful information can be obtained from the website of the Food Standards Agency: www.food.gov.uk.

Health and safety

Related to the issue of food hygiene is that of health and safety – and there is a certain amount of overlap.

A sandwich-coffee bar isn't the same as a machine tool factory but there are still lots of ways, unrelated to food, that people can come to grief. And if they do then you could find yourself on the receiving end of a claim for damages.

As with food hygiene there is a mass of legislation. It would be completely unrealistic for you to become familiar with it all. However, as with food hygiene a lot of it boils down to common sense and the authorities will always be available to give advice on anything you're not sure about.

The principal statute on the subject is The Health and Safety at Work Act 1974. You are responsible for the health and safety of everyone affected by your business. This covers:

◆ employees
◆ tradespeople working in your premises
◆ people visiting your premises – i.e. customers
◆ people outside your premises – e.g. people affected by emissions from your shop.

The first thing to point out is that if you have employees you must **register** with your local council – usually with the Environmental Health Department. Contact your local environmental health officer to obtain details of how to do this in your area.

Health and safety policy

You should also have a policy on health and safety. If you have five or more employees it must be in writing and the document must be brought to the attention of all employees. Clearly what the government principally has in mind with such legislation is the safety of people working with dangerous or complex machinery in factories or on building sites, etc. However, there are most certainly areas of relevance to the proprietor of a sandwich bar, for instance:

◆ what to do in the event of an accident
◆ not leaving objects in places where people could trip over them
◆ location of first aid kit
◆ having a system of work which allows for the free circulation of staff
◆ safe storage of knives.

I would suggest that such matters be included in a section of the staff handbook, thus avoiding the need to burden your staff with yet another document. In fact, you could combine the staff handbook with the written particulars of employment (or 'contract of employment') and just have one document to cover everything.

Risk assessment

In order to be fully aware of potential problem areas you should carry out a risk assessment. In an average sized shop unit you will probably have become aware of most likely difficulties in the course of acquiring and fitting out the place. Some you might not become aware of until you are up and running.

> We found that some drinks cans were delivered around lunch time. This meant that we had a sweating delivery driver laden down with four or five trays of juice cans backing into the shop at a time when there were lots of customers coming, going and queuing. Clearly a recipe for disaster. We simply told the company concerned that deliveries would have to take place before 11.00am or after 3.00pm.

Either way it is your duty to make sure that the staff are aware of problems and how to deal with them. Remember, you can't assume that a new employee will have such things explained to them by existing employees – it's your responsibility.

Employer's liability insurance

You must have employer's liability insurance. This can be arranged by your insurance adviser. A current certificate confirming that the cover is in place must be displayed on the premises.

Staff training

I have touched on the subject of staff training previously. Your obligation also extends to making sure that staff are aware of any relevant health and safety procedures. You are also supposed to monitor them to see that they are getting it right. In an operation the size of a sandwich-coffee bar this will occur naturally in the course of the work, but you should be aware of your responsibilities nonetheless. There is a poster called 'Health and Safety Law: What You Should Know'. This should either be put up on the wall or given to staff individually. It can be obtained from the Health and Safety Executive (0845 345 0055).

Another area of responsibility is fire precautions. In the case of a sandwich-coffee bar these are fairly limited and will probably amount to having a fire extinguisher in good working order and a couple of fire blankets. Contact your local fire prevention officer who will be happy to visit the premises and advise you on any other appropriate measures.

> Beware of salesmen who come round trying to get you to sign contracts for the purchase and maintenance of fire extinguishers. In my experience people who operate this way charge substantially more than the companies you contact through Yellow Pages.

Other responsibilities

Many of the other matters you are responsible for amount to little more than common sense. They include:

◆ adequate clean **toilet** facilities
◆ comfortable **temperatures** to work in (at least 13°C where people are active – this certainly applies to a sandwich bar)
◆ adequate **lighting**
◆ a **rest area** – though this need not be a separate room
◆ **first aid** facilities
◆ an **accident book** in which all accidents and 'near misses' should be recorded.

Under the RIDDOR rules (Reporting of Injuries, Diseases and Dangerous Occurrences Regulations) you are required to report:

◆ serious **injuries or deaths** related to your business
◆ **dangerous incidents**, for instance if a piece of electrical equipment suddenly went on fire
◆ **employee absences** of more than three days as a result of an accident
◆ the certification by a doctor of **specified occupational diseases** (detailed in a booklet called 'RIDDOR 95' obtainable from the Environmental Health Department).

In the event of any of these things happening you should contact your EHO.

The local authority – usually the Environmental Health Department – is in charge of health and safety. If you have any queries at all you should always contact your local EHO in the first instance.

The Health and Safety Executive (HSE) provides a range of free and paid-for publications via their website www.hse.gov.uk or telephone their helpline: 0845 345 0055

Labelling

There are complicated regulations which apply to the labelling of many foodstuffs *including sandwiches in certain circumstances*. They currently derive from a 1997 EU Directive and are known as the 'QUID Regulations'. Your life will doubtless be enriched by the knowledge that 'QUID' stands for Quantitative Ingredient Declarations. The regulations aim to enhance and assist consumer choice when buying food by providing information about the ingredients of what they are buying. The main result is that you have to include on the label what percentage of all of the ingredients the principal ingredients constitute, the principal ingredients being the things that influence the consumer to buy a food product in the first place – e.g. the egg and cress in an egg and cress sandwich. So if the rules apply, the label has to say 'Eggs 36%, Cress 4%' or whatever.

However, you can relax – the regulations do not apply to sandwiches sold on the premises where they were made, or on other premises owned by the manufacturer. In other words, if you have two outlets and you make sandwiches in one to be sold in the other then the regulations will not apply.

It is important to be aware of the regulations if you buy in pre-packed sandwiches from a large sandwich manufacturer – in this case the regulations will certainly apply. If the manufacturer has not put on the correct labelling then you the retailer will be in breach of the regulations. Similarly if you decide there is a market for you in making sandwiches for other, separate outlets then the sandwiches you supply to them must be correctly labelled. To obtain more information and guidance about this issue you should contact your local council and ask to speak to a **trading standards officer**.

Organic food

Lots of people like the idea of being able to describe the things they sell as organic. Organic products are usually more expensive, which can be a turn-off for customers, but as they become more common, then no doubt prices will come down a bit. There are restrictions concerning the use of the term "organic" to describe any of your products and for further information you should visit the website of the Department for Environment Food and Rural Affairs (DEFRA) www.defra.gov.uk

The strictures do not apply if you buy in pre-prepared sandwiches with organic ingredients and sell them in their original packaging. Similarly they do not apply if you use some organic ingredients but do not advertise the fact.

CHAPTER TEN

Getting Up and Running

Before opening

The deal's done, you've got the keys – now the real pressure begins. Your aim is to get trading as soon as possible and see some money travelling in the other direction. By now a lot of important decisions will have been made – who's going to supply the coffee, which cash and carry you're going to use, who's going to fit out the shop and so on. Don't worry though, there's still plenty to do!

Creating interest

People are always interested to know what kind of new venture is going to be opening on their patch. The day you get the keys, go into the shop and blank out the windows with Windolene or something similar leaving enough space for a poster advertising that a quality sandwich-coffee bar will be opening shortly. At this stage don't tie yourself down to a date. Even if you take over an existing business you may well have to close it down for a while to re-decorate or upgrade fittings or equipment.

Maintaining momentum

The people who are going to fit out your shop or deliver equipment to you don't have the same financial imperative as you. A couple of days here or there won't make any difference to them – but it might to you. You must stay on top of things. Even if everything goes like clockwork (which it won't) this will be hard work.

Unless you have superhuman powers you will not be able to keep all the information you need to process in your head. You must have a do list, a timetable, a flow chart or some kind of combination of all of them – whatever works for you. You should also have with you at all times a list of the key people involved from the bank to the plumber plus their phone numbers.

Even when one particular job has started you must not assume that it will be completed in the shortest possible time. Tradespeople are usually juggling a number of jobs at any one time. That's their problem. Yours is being able to open at the earliest opportunity. So whether it's installing kitchen units or delivery dates for fridges you have to be at people constantly, checking that things are going according to plan, nipping problems in the bud, pressing for completion or delivery dates and generally keeping the momentum going.

Staff training days

You will need to spend time training staff in virtual trading conditions before you open. Try to make this as real as possible. Invite friends or family to be 'customers'. Obviously the idea is to prepare for the real thing.

Publicity surrounding the opening

Local advertising

The best form of advertising is a talkative happy customer. However, you want to help your cause in the early stages by raising awareness as much as possible.

One of the advantages of a sandwich-coffee bar is that your potential market comes from a fairly small hinterland. Accordingly you don't need to spread your advertising net too wide. Once you know to within a few days when you will open, you should distribute advertising literature to every place which might be a potential source of business within a radius of half a mile or so. It might be a good idea to include a simple map with 'We are here' emblazoned on it. When I say distribute I mean getting out on foot and pushing things through letter-boxes or under the doors of:

◆ **Nearby shops** – including other take-aways (some of the staff at the pizza place next door to us come to us for sandwiches).
◆ **Offices** – almost certainly the best bet for business.
◆ **Colleges, government departments, halls of residence, courts, police stations, etc.** Try to see if you can get advertisements placed on a notice board or in staff rest areas. These places may well have their own subsidised food, but don't be put off by some sniffy receptionist who tells you this. The fact is people like a change. And even if they only come to you once a week – that's an extra 52 sandwiches and drinks each year – per head.

If you have a menu it should, of course, be ready by this time. Your advertising literature should include a menu and a small flier giving the actual opening date and details of any opening special offers.

Press advertising

You can arrange for an advertising feature to appear in your local evening paper. There's no doubt that such advertisements can make a memorable splash. But the problem is that they will mainly reach areas far away from your site which will be of little or no commercial relevance to you. And they don't come cheap. For the small independent they are of doubtful value.

Opening attractions

The point here is to do anything lawful which makes the locals aware of your presence.

- **Special offers** – for instance, a free coffee with every sandwich, the first 25 sandwiches half price. It should be heavily promoted on the sandwich board outside and possibly detailed in a flier delivered through the night (what, were you planning to get some sleep?) to the places you delivered the other advertising literature to a few days before.
- **Hire** some entertainment such as a jazz band to play in the street outside the shop. This one could be a bit of a damp squib if it rains. Not such a good idea in winter.
- Get some impressive **balloons or bunting** and cover the frontage of the shop in them.
- **Invite some friends** to sit in the shop eating sandwiches, looking as if they are enjoying themselves.
- Get someone to **dress up as a sandwich and hand out menus** to all passers-by (possibly with free sandwich samples as well).
- **Invite** Julia Roberts and Robbie Williams for the day. This would be expensive because you would have to meet the cost of policing the crowds who would turn up.

Seriously though, use your imagination.

> *One word of caution:* not everybody thinks this kind of publicity is necessarily a good idea. The argument goes that perhaps it would be best for a new business to work itself in for a few days at a low level of trading. This way initial problems can be ironed out when the shop is fairly quiet. Getting things wrong under the gaze of a crowd of potential regulars might not give you the ideal start.

After opening

The weeks after you open will be a blur. After the launch, once patterns start to emerge and the whole thing starts to feel established, you have, as captain of the ship, to keep it on course and in good order. There will be times when a firm hand on the rudder is needed.

Maintain an objective overview

If you work hands-on in the shop it can be very tempting to bury yourself in work. If you do this you may fail to notice things which aren't working. You may also come to identify yourself too much with the other members of staff. You mustn't forget that you are the boss. You must learn to stand back, as a painter does, and be prepared to make changes as necessary. You must try to *look at the shop from the customer's point of view* and assess whether they could have any legitimate cause for complaint. This can be difficult because it may mean telling people to do things differently; people with whom you have shared the excitement of getting the new venture off the ground. Examples of the kind of thing I mean, particularly in the early stages could be:

◆ telling staff to make up sandwiches more quickly
◆ telling staff to adopt a different manner with customers
◆ getting rid of staff who are not working out
◆ discontinuing a particular sandwich, despite your own enthusiasm, because it's not selling.

As weeks become months the issues change; they become more long-term.

Keep an eye on what the opposition and the industry in general is doing

This can be important both for identifying new trends and also for checking what prices are being charged for the kinds of things you sell.

Make sure that the shop continues to look good

Once a few months go by all that beautiful fresh decor will start to show the first signs of tattiness. Try to stand back from your work of art every now and then and assess it objectively, like a customer coming in for the first time. Maintain the place in as good condition as possible and make good any marks or stains. You will need to redecorate every three years or so. Financially it's a strain but it's all tax deductible and it creates a good impression for customers: 'If that's how they look after the property I bet they're hot on health and hygiene'.

Introduce new ideas

The introduction of a new sandwich, hot snack or pastry is a good justification for eye-catching changes to your sandwich board and for any other advertising you can think of. It also gives out the message that you are innovative. You also have to accept that some ideas might not work.

> I was once on holiday in Paris when an idea came to me: all day continental breakfasts. Brilliant. Easy. It was just a case of putting together a few things, some of which we were selling already, in a neat package and buying some inexpensive trays. We reckoned we could charge £2.50 and make about £1 profit per breakfast. If we sold, say, 25 a day that'd be £375 a week, delivering a profit of £150 a week or about £7,800 a year. A not insignificant contribution to our annual figures from one simple idea. We sold one breakfast in the first week and buried the idea a week or so after that. Two clichéd sayings apply here: C'est la vie; nothing ventured nothing gained.

Be aware of new trends

In recent times somebody has come up with the idea of a 'conewich.' It's in the shape of an ice-cream cone and is stuffed with normal sandwich-type ingredients. And have you heard of functional foods and nutraceuticals? These are products which purport to have health promoting qualities over and above their nutritional value and include such things as cholesterol-lowering margarines, and breads which are thought to reduce menopausal symptoms. Concerns over their regulation and the whole notion of 'Frankenstein' foods may limit their acceptance.

There are new things coming out all the time and it's good to be aware of what's going on and what the new thinking is, even if you don't take advantage of them all.

Advertising

As I said before the best form of advertising is a talkative satisfied customer with lots of friends, acquaintances and business colleagues. Given the localised nature of sandwich bars more conventional advertising is inappropriate and expensive.

However, there are exceptions:

◆ **Local radio stations** which are based in your particular locality and whose target audience is likely to include a lot of your customers or potential customers. The most obvious example of this is a student radio station. The charges are usually very reasonable.

◆ **Local advertising newspapers.** The point is that these are distributed to residents and traders in your neighbourhood and will be seen by a good proportion of your target audience. Again, charges are usually low.

◆ *Yellow Pages* – if you decide to go in for outside catering or delivering sandwiches. I shall say more about these in Chapter Eleven.

◆ **Mailshots** – if you decide to introduce something new: a new sandwich, wraps, a microwavable hot dish and so on, you could use this as an excuse to send e-mails or deliver fliers to nearby shops and offices. These can be printed from your PC and delivered by hand, so any costs will be minimal. They remind people that you are there and might reach people who missed your opening publicity.

You will often see people putting balloons out or providing special offers on their **first anniversary** – it's an excuse to advertise and draws attention to the fact that you've survived what will probably be the most difficult year. Funnily enough people don't tend to put out balloons on their second and subsequent birthdays.

> **Follow your instincts regarding publicity. The aim is to become an established and respected part of your local scene.**

Holidays

You may well find that a holiday in the first year will be out of the question. However, I don't think it's a good idea to get into that martyred state of mind which some small businesspeople do which results in them never getting a break. For some people it seems to become a badge of honour.

Whilst it is true that you will be pivotal to the operation, I am not aware of any statistical evidence supporting the conclusion that total disaster and destruction will be the inevitable consequence of you taking a holiday.

The fact is we all need a break sometimes. We owe it to ourselves and our families. It may be that shorter holidays would be a good compromise – a week in the sun or a short city break may be appealing. Bear in mind also that there are quite a number of organisations that give Air Miles if you buy their products. And there are some credit card companies that give Air Miles, so you could get double miles. It really doesn't take long to build up a worthwhile balance. Air Miles can be used towards package holidays as well as just flights. *You've got to spend the money so why not turn it to your advantage? Make a virtue out of a necessity.*

The biggest problem for the smaller operation is dealing with the question: Who will run the show when I'm away? This can be especially difficult if you do any food prep at home. The best answer is to think about holidays well in advance. Consider which member of staff might be best able to look after things when you are away. Talk to them early. Make it clear there will be some kind of bonus. Is there a relation who would be prepared to come into the house and do some cooking? For a week, could you manage to do without the things which are usually prepared at home, allowing you to rely on suppliers who can deliver to the shop? I think it's best to find a way to do this.

If you can't work anything out you have two options, each of which is undesirable:

1. Don't take a holiday.
2. Close the shop for a week or two.

The first is a bad idea for the reasons already stated.

The second isn't problem-free either. It is hugely appealing because it means you can head off to the sun without worrying about what's going on back at the ranch – because nothing's going on. A lot of well-established family businesses do this. However, although regulars are loyal up to a point, they are also fickle up to a point. **And the fact is there are many sandwich-coffee bar alternatives on offer.** Some of your regulars will check out other places. Will they come back? Probably most of them will but not necessarily on the day you re-open. They won't have your holiday dates in their diaries. This will mean that in addition to the loss of income when you are away, it will be a week or so before you get back up to speed.

Another point is that if you close the shop then, of course, your staff will have to take the same holiday as you, and you will have to fork out holiday pay – so it's a double financial whammy. *As always, lots of factors for you to weigh up.*

A lot of places now join up the Christmas and New Year holidays to give themselves a decent break at a time of the year which tends to be quieter anyway. Good thinking.

Price rises

Getting the price right is not an exact science. The cost of some of your supplies will almost certainly go up at various times of the year. This will not happen in an ordered way. It could be chocolate bars from the cash and carry, Brie from your cheese supplier or cucumbers in winter. In addition, you will find that other sandwich-coffee bars in your area will impose price rises from time to time. You might also negotiate the odd discount (always be on the look-out for such opportunities and don't be bashful) and occasionally prices do actually come down. However, overall, there is a constant upward pressure on prices.

Your task is to be aware of what is happening. In my experience you just start to become aware of the need to raise prices. Competition is tough nowadays so there can be a temptation to leave prices alone for fear of losing business. The trouble is if you do this your profit margin will go down. If this goes on for too long questions will arise as to the viability of the business.

Price rises are inevitable and necessary but there is no right answer to the question: 'How much should I increase prices by?' You have to weigh up the relevant factors and make a decision. My experience suggests that a price rise once a year is about right.

> **Don't be timid about it. You're providing a good service and you are entitled to be paid at a level that delivers a reasonable profit.**

Remember that in arriving at a figure you should try to anticipate any increases in the next year – difficult, of course, but you don't want to be behind the game and always feeling that your prices are on the low side.

Another issue is how to tell your customers. There isn't really a nice way of doing this. I suggest a notice prominently displayed *inside* the shop (why advertise negatively to the world at large?). It should simply say that due to increases in the costs of supplies you have found it necessary to increase prices – there's no need to apologise.

Tell your staff to be sensitive to situations where a regular brings exactly the right money each day (we have a few of these). Let him off with the price rise on the first day. Leave the sign up for three days at the most. Assuming you are delivering a good product at a reasonable price you will be pleasantly surprised at how little reaction (adverse or otherwise) you will get from customers.

Whatever you do, don't feel guilty!

Factors affecting trade

Keep notes of factors affecting trading patterns. One of your most important jobs is to monitor the business closely, especially in the first year. This self-evidently makes sense. It will take a full year's trading for the different patterns to become clear and sudden unexpected changes can be unsettling during this period. To make things easier in subsequent years make notes – somewhere you look at regularly, financial records being the obvious choice – of anything which has a palpable effect on the level of the daily take (up or down). *These records help you to predict and be prepared for increases or decreases in demand in subsequent years.* The important points will be different for every operation. Here are some examples:

◆ the day students break up for holidays
◆ local fairs or festivals which bring lots of people into your area
◆ very bad weather conditions (helps to explain figures which are out of line)
◆ bank/office/local holidays – there seem to be more and more of these
◆ the first few days of the tourists hitting town in a big way
◆ when the Christmas party season starts – and your business starts to suffer as a result.

Increasing your income

There are only three ways to increase your income:

1. increasing turnover
2. making savings
3. a combination of 1 and 2.

Without becoming too obsessive about it (a common affliction amongst small businesspeople!), increasing the money you make should be an important ongoing element of your role. In general the people who work for you will not see this as part of their job.

One of the things that struck me about our first business was how quickly we got to a situation where we were bringing in roughly the same amount of money most days. There were seasonal fluctuations, of course, but the variation from day to day was remarkably small. This used to puzzle me. We were in a particularly busy part of town with a variety of sources of business so, my reasoning went, the figures would probably fluctuate unpredictably from day to day. But it just doesn't work like this.

This is a double-edged phenomenon. Assuming the level is sufficient to make you an acceptable profit then you appreciate that stability – it's like a heartbeat. On the other hand it can be frustrating because it becomes a kind of glass ceiling which is difficult to break through – which means you feel there isn't much prospect of getting a pay rise. You can just keep working hard, producing a quality product and hope that you attract more business. This may well work but once you've reached your cruising height, the increases will be small.

Increasing turnover

To make more substantial increases you will have to expand the business and branch out into other areas. I will deal with these areas in more detail in Chapter Eleven. However, there are two ways of increasing turnover without altering or expanding the nature of the operation to any great extent:

1. Attracting business during dead times

Sandwich-coffee bars do most of their business during a hectic period of one and a half to two hours. It follows there are times when business is slack. This doesn't mean you're not occupied but it does leave scope for finding ways of bringing more people in.

More and more people are getting into the way of eating and drinking outside the home. In the past it might have been a sandwich at lunchtime, a few drinks after work and the odd office restaurant lunch. Now, despite the hectic lifestyles we hear about all the time, people have the time, money and inclination to indulge themselves at all times of the day. In many areas the home-prepared packed lunch has been consigned to history. this is good news for you. *Your job is to catch the customer's eye.*

a. Breakfast trade

If you're going to do this properly you may have to open earlier because people will want breakfast on their way to work. They will not have much time so the service has to be quick.

You should introduce some new items which are specifically breakfast-oriented such as bowls of muesli, porridge or prunes with cream. It may be a good idea to invest in a hot plate so that some things, for instance croissants with scrambled eggs or bacon rolls, are ready to go. As always with anything new, do as much street advertising as possible to raise awareness.

Apparently some office people have such busy hectic lives nowadays that they don't have time for breakfast in the morning. It could be very appealing to them to pick up something to eat on the way to work. When they reach their office they can then settle down and eat their 'deskfast' while checking their e-mails, reading their snail-mail and checking their diary.

If you are going to target the breakfast market seriously make sure you will still have sufficient time to prepare sandwiches for the shelf in good time. There is no point whatever in attracting more customers in the early morning at the expense of the service you deliver to others at the most important time.

b. Mid morning/afternoon

As with the breakfast trade you should introduce some new things to sell specifically aimed at these slots. The obvious things are cakes and pastries. There really are some excellent sweet things available now, often from small patissiers some of whom may have come from France. You can also get frozen products from the big suppliers. In my experience these do not tend to be so good – heavy and sugary – but of course there will be less waste. Home-made is usually popular so why not try out some new recipes, assuming you intend to do some food prep at home? As always, new developments should be advertised as much as possible.

If you have not done so already you should make your seating area as attractive as possible. It may seem a small point but have newspapers or magazines which are likely to appeal to your particular customers. When I go to my dentist the waiting room is full of magazines about fly fishing and sailing. This no doubt reflects the hobbies of one of my torturers but such magazines hold no interest for me. In our sandwich bar the favourites are *Hello* and *Private Eye*. *Subscribe to magazines you and your customers like and charge it to the business.*

Some of the bigger chains now try to recreate the atmosphere of a comfortable living room: leather armchairs and so on. There is plenty of scope for this and you might even add the odd witty touch such as a standard lamp.

2. Persuading customers to spend more

The most obvious way of doing this is loyalty cards. You print cards which are appropriately marked each time somebody buys a sandwich. When they have bought six they get one free – or something of the sort.

In most cities there are schemes you can buy into whereby you pay an annual fee to an organisation which then advertises its subscribers all over town. Under this scheme you will have to give some discount to customers. So you pay to join *and* you give discount. In other words, such schemes will have to bring in a lot of new business to justify themselves.

Making savings

This is largely a matter of common sense. If you find you are having to throw out smoked turkey or venison then order less. If it still happens you will have to consider discontinuing a particular line. This will usually happen with the less common things – I'm afraid the British are still a bit unadventurous, though this will vary from place to place. This is particularly unfortunate if you are trying to appear sophisticated and cosmopolitan.

> In my own case it's still a source of disappointment that we found it necessary to stop selling taramasalata, seedless grapes and tomato – in my view one of the best sandwiches we did. The paying public didn't agree.

There is one other way of keeping costs down and that is *keeping stocks at a low level*. When going to the cash and carry or the supermarket it's all too easy to buy in bigger quantities than necessary to meet your immediate needs on the basis that you'll need it sooner or later.

> **This is bad thinking. You're parting with hard-earned cash, some of which could be spending a bit more time in your bank account. You have to go to the cash and carry and the supermarket on a regular basis so just get what you need and keep your stocks lean – though not emaciated. Get the balance right.**

Of course, if a supplier is offering a particularly good price for something that will keep for ages then it may well make sense to buy a lot at one go.

Ordering supplies

You'll save a lot of hassle if you develop a good system of ordering. Just imagine what kind of morning you'll have if you arrive in the shop at 7.30 to find there are no rolls because somebody forgot to order them.

- Have set times when ordering is done.
- Have a system of double-checking.
- Ensure it is clearly understood who is responsible for ordering. Don't assume that someone will get round to it at some point.
- For those orders placed by phone ensure that up-to-date phone numbers and the name of the person to speak to are clearly displayed on the wall near the phone – not under a pile of papers somewhere.
- Set up standing orders with suppliers for items where the requirement is the same every day. Always remember to change the standing order at busier or quieter times.
- Have plentiful supplies of order forms for your various suppliers. This means you just have to tick boxes rather than write things out. These can be produced on a PC.
- If possible try to place orders by fax or e-mail. This way you have a record of what you ordered. It also saves you or your employee's time trying to get through to people by phone.

List of staff, contacts and tradespeople

You never know when you'll need to get hold of, for example:

- **A member of staff** – you discover at 8 o'clock in the evening that the cash takings for the day are £30 less than the till reading
- **A contact at the bakery** – the weather forecast's dreadful and you want to reduce the bread order at 10 o'clock in the evening, though in this case you will doubtless be talking to an answering machine.
- **A plumber** – there's a leak in the toilet.

You should have a list prominently displayed in the shop. This should, of course, include your phone and mobile phone numbers. The list should be regularly updated as staff leave or you stop using particular suppliers or tradespeople.

Needless to say, the easiest way to have a list like this is stored on a PC. It can be updated with a few taps on the keypad and fresh copies can be printed when the old ones become dog-eared.

Bookkeeping and tax

At the risk of stating the obvious, in order to comply with taxation laws it is necessary to record all the financial intromissions of your business to enable your liability to tax to be assessed. Not only that but financial records must be retained for around six years. It follows that bookkeeping is an important part of any business. You should have a good, user friendly system in place before you start. The really important thing thereafter is to get into the habit of entering information in your records on a regular basis.

> **If bookkeeping is new to you, consider going on a brief course which will teach you the basics. Such courses are widely available from colleges and other organisations and are advertised in the press. Your accountant will also be able to give you advice on suitable courses.**

A good bookkeeping system should provide you with a clear and easy-to-follow analysis of the money you earn and where it goes. Systems are based on spreadsheets with columns for the various ways money comes in and goes out. This means, for instance, that you will have a column for motor expenses, another for bank repayments and another for VAT and so on.

Apart from the legal obligation to record such information it is very helpful for you to be able to see at a glance what you are spending on particular items each month. In addition, you should be able to make comparisons with previous years. It is also necessary to carry out reconciliations between the money which is recorded coming into the business and your bank account.

You can buy bookkeeping systems from stationers' shops in which you hand-write your entries. Many such systems will be adequate for the needs of the small business. However, very serious consideration should be given to using a PC with a bookkeeping programme. Apart from bookkeeping, a PC can carry out a huge range of invaluable functions for your business which will save you money in numerous ways. I detailed many of these in Chapter Seven. Consider these additional advantages:

◆ When entering data, you don't need to worry about making mistakes which you have to messily rub out – just press the delete key and do it again.

- Once the information is entered you can play around with it and analyse it.
- Whilst you do have to create some space in the house for the computer, monitor, printer and scanner, you will not have to keep so many paper records.
- Becoming familiar with a PC will equip you with what nowadays has become a basic skill in the workplace.
- It is possible to enable your till to 'talk' to your PC. This means that the information keyed in by you and your staff when serving customers during the day is available to you on your PC. The effect is to cut down considerably the amount of feeding in of data you have to do.
- Communication by e-mail is becoming more common, making a PC even more desirable. It will be possible for customers to place orders by e-mail.
- Assuming you buy your computer at the outset the cost can be included in your initial loan. It is a good idea to include as many big items as possible at this stage. Once you're up and running you want to keep extra loan commitments to a minimum.
- If you have any queries regarding tax, employment law, health and safety, etc. you can visit the website of the appropriate government department for information.

Let's take a look at the taxes which are likely to be of relevance to you as a self-employed person.

Income tax

This is the main tax. Self-employed people are responsible for paying their own tax ('schedule D'). Calculations are made for tax years which run from 6th April. Broadly speaking your tax calculation for any year will be based on your trading profits for the accounting year which ends in the same tax year. Adjustments have to be made to reflect the fact that your trading year will not coincide exactly with the tax year.

A tax return will be issued in April. You can calculate your tax liability yourself, get HMRC to do it or pay an accountant to do it for you. Trading accounts provide the basis of your tax liability. They are usually, though not necessarily, prepared by accountants and are generally in two parts:

- the trading profit and loss account – effectively a summary of the financial transactions of the business
- the balance sheet – this shows the assets and liabilities of the business.

The way the system now works you make payments on account of tax on 31st January and 31st July. Any balance outstanding has to be paid in the following January together with the first payment on account for the following tax year. If you employ accountants there shouldn't be any shortfall of any significance. If there is they will have some questions to answer, *assuming, of course, that you provided them with all necessary information.*

You can prepare your own profit and loss accounts and complete your own tax returns. You will certainly save some money on accountants' fees if you do this. There are various publications available which will give you guidance.

However, do you feel confident about working out what allowances you can claim, the most tax-efficient way of splitting up the share of profit between yourself and your spouse and what steps to take to keep your capital gains tax liability to a minimum?

And what if you are unlucky enough to be singled out for a tax inspection? Wouldn't you rather have an expert on your side able to deal with the points raised? There is in my view a very strong argument in favour of letting an expert attend to this side of things on your behalf.

> **The main point is that an accountant will (or certainly should)**
> **ensure that you pay as little tax as legally possible.**

Your accountant will also give you valuable advice when setting up your business in the first place. In my view these services justify the fees, which are, of course, all tax deductible.

But remember – even though you engage accountants there is still scope for saving money. By keeping neat, detailed and readily comprehensible records and associated documents (receipts, till rolls, etc.) and giving them to your accountants on time, you will be doing work which is within your capability, and which it would be wasteful to pay an accountant to do on your behalf. Your accountant should charge you less if you provide them with spreadsheets, etc.

National Insurance

It may be called insurance but to all intents and purposes it is a tax. Self-employed people are liable to pay two classes of contribution:

◆ **Class 2:** a flat rate contribution which is currently £2.40 per week. It provides money for things like Incapacity Benefit, Maternity Allowance and the Retirement Pension.

The obligation to pay Class 2 contributions is personal. It is not a business liability.

◆ **Class 4:** based on a percentage of annual profits between a lower and upper profit level. The levels are set each year by the Chancellor. For the year 2008–2009 the levels are:

percentage rate – 8%

lower profit level – £5,715

upper profit level – £43,875

Payments are collected along with your schedule D income tax. According to the official blurb Class 4 contributions do not entitle you to any benefit, but they do help to share the cost of funding the benefits to all self-employed people in the fairest way. Now you know.

Value Added Tax (VAT)

If you are in business and your taxable supplies to customers exceed or are likely to exceed a set limit in a year then you have to register with HMRC. The limit is currently £70,000 but the figure is reviewed annually. Once you register you then have to charge your customers VAT on vatable items. The standard rate of VAT is currently 20%.

For sandwich bars the situation is not totally straightforward since some of the things you will sell are zero-rated – so you have to know which things to charge VAT on and which not to.

◆ Convenience pre-packed foods such as crisps, confectionery and drinks are subject to VAT at the standard rate. So are hot food items such as toasted sandwiches, teas and coffees.

◆ Cold sandwiches, cakes and fruit are zero-rated. **However, if people sit in then VAT at the standard rate becomes chargeable.** Accordingly, although it is rather tedious, you do have to ask people if they will be sitting in or taking away if they are buying zero-rated items. Given that you are providing seating, paying for the heating, lighting, etc. you may want to consider charging people who sit in an extra premium on top of VAT to reflect this.

You charge VAT on the relevant items you have sold (output tax) and then have to account for it to HMRC. You can, however, set off any VAT you have incurred buying things for the business (input tax) in your quarterly returns.

One of the questions for a new business is when to register. Clearly you will not reach a figure of £70,000 for some time. However, you do want to be able to reclaim the large amounts of VAT you will have spent on your start-up costs. And it is quite permissible to register even if your turnover is below the limit. My view is that it is to your advantage to register at the earliest opportunity. The rules state that, while you can register before you make taxable supplies – i.e. sell sandwiches – you do have to have 'started a business'. This is clearly open to interpretation but at the very least I think there is an argument that this should include the period when you are doing all the initial research. Opening a bank account and having some headed paper printed will help to bolster this argument.

It may even be possible to reclaim the VAT spent on research costs – i.e. visiting lots of sandwich bars to try them out, perhaps travelling to London to check out the scene there. I understand this is a grey area. Keep all receipts and include the VAT in the section for VAT spent on supplies – input tax – and do a covering letter to HMRC arguing your case. HMRC have a national helpline: 0845 010 9000.

> **Keep personal and business money transactions separate right**
> **from the start. Keep receipts for all business type payments and as soon as**
> **practicable open a separate business bank account.**

Tax contingency

As a self-employed person you will be responsible for paying schedule D tax twice a year on 31st January and 31st July. You will probably also have to make quarterly VAT returns. To begin with, the latter can be rather a pleasant experience since your heavy start-up costs will almost certainly mean that you will be due a substantial amount of VAT back. However, VAT will soon become just another regular payment. As will the tax and National Insurance you have to account for on behalf of your employees.

If you don't make some contingency for these payments then you aren't living in the real world. You will be at risk of labouring under the misapprehension that your income is at a higher level than it really is.

Make a virtue out of a necessity. Open a tax efficient savings account such as an ISA which may only require one week's notice for withdrawals. Pay in a little regularly. I know it's a counsel of perfection but it really does make sense.

Borrowing money to pay tax should be avoided if at all possible. It is an indication that the business is not generating sufficient profit to stand on its own two feet.

If you do not have a private pension you should also give serious consideration to this. The state pension will never provide more than the most basic and frankly inadequate level of support. The sooner you take out a private pension the lower will be the premiums and the greater the eventual benefits. However, in recent years pension funds have performed poorly and their future is not as rosily reassuring as once appeared to be the case. It may be a good idea to consider another way of investing for the future as well. The obvious choice here is property.

Business rates

Business rates constitute a local property-based tax applicable to commercial properties. This tax is entirely separate from the council tax payable in respect of your house. Rateable values are based on market rents and are revalued every five years. Most people pay their rates by instalments over the course of a year.

PAYE

Assuming you employ staff you will be legally responsible for deducting income tax and Class 1 National Insurance contributions from their pay under the Pay As You Earn Scheme (PAYE). The main points about your responsibilities are:

◆ The money has to be sent to the HM Revenue and Customs Accounts Office. Payment can be made quarterly if your average monthly payments of tax and National Insurance are less than £1,500.

◆ You must tell your tax office at the end of the year how much each employee has earned and how much tax and National Insurance you have deducted.

◆ You must provide your staff with payslips showing their earnings, tax and National Insurance contributions, deductions made for the year and any benefits provided.

◆ You have to pay tax credits through the payroll unless a couple has opted for a non-working or self-employed partner to receive the credit. You do not, however, have to calculate an individual's tax credit entitlement – HMRC will do this.

Some businesses pay their accountants to work out PAYE, National Insurance and VAT for them – they will no doubt arrive at the correct figures. But do you really want to pay them to do the easy stuff as well as the more complicated things? VAT returns are straightforward and HMRC will be happy to assist you in the early stages. The situation is similar in the case of PAYE and National Insurance. Indeed, there are computer programs which you can subscribe to which effectively do the work for you. For a modest outlay you are sent up-to-date software when the figures change and you also have access to a helpline.

> There is quite a lot to take in, especially if you have never been in business for yourself before. But the good news is that there is a great deal of help on hand from the relevant government bodies. After all, it is not just in your interests to get things right – it will also save them a lot of trouble too. As part of your initial research, visit the business start up section of the HM Revenue & Customs website www.hmrc.gov.uk/startingup/index.htm which contains a great deal of useful information. They also have a helpline 0845 915 4515.

Registering with the authorities

When you start a business in a self-employed capacity you must register with the authorities within three months. You need to inform:

◆ the HM Revenue and Customs National Insurance Contributions Office (you will also require to register for VAT purposes if your turnover is likely to exceed £70,000).
◆ your local Tax Office

The good news is that all of this has been made very easy. There is one form, which is part of the publication 'Starting Your Own Business?' which you complete and send off.

In addition, assuming you are going to employ staff, you must contact the New Employers' Helpline on 0845 60 70 143. Lines are open Monday to Friday 8 am to 8 pm and Saturday and Sunday 8 am to 5 pm. You will be asked for basic details and will then be sent a starter pack containing information on the payment of tax and National Insurance contributions through the PAYE system.

There are local Business Support Teams up and down the country which provide support on all aspects of the payroll to new and small employers. They run half-day workshops on a wide variety of topics relevant to the small business. You will be put in touch with your local team after you phone the New Employers' Helpline.

CHAPTER ELEVEN

Beyond the Basic Concept

You may feel that having got your little empire up on its feet the last thing you want to know about is taking things further. Fair enough. You will have plenty to keep you busy – especially if you work hands-on in the shop every day. However, if your first experience of running a sandwich bar whets your appetite for more, there are plenty of ideas to consider.

Outside catering

This is the most obvious expansion route. You will find that some customers will ask you to provide sandwiches and drinks for an office do from time to time. This is simple to cater for given a little notice. However, what you have to consider is whether you want to go out looking for this kind of business. The great advantage is that you are really just doing more of what you're in business to do anyway. To do it properly though you really need to be organised.

- ◆ **Create a separate outside catering menu.** This should offer per head prices at various levels depending on what extras (drinks, cakes, fruit, etc.) are provided. Circulate these to local businesses and have them available in the shop. You should probably have a minimum order number.
- ◆ **Get the pricing right.** Your prices should be worked out to reflect the fact that you are getting a larger than normal order which is known in advance (i.e. knock them down a bit) and the fact that you will probably have to deliver (i.e. add on a bit).
- ◆ **Put up a prominent sign advertising your outside catering service.** This should be clearly visible from the street. Consider advertising in the *Yellow Pages* or local newspapers. It's pricey but if you don't it can be difficult to get yourself known beyond your own immediate area.
- ◆ **Have a system for taking orders.** This is absolutely vital. If somebody phones with an order every member of staff must know exactly what to do. *You must have a pro forma order form which includes a space for the name and telephone number of the person*

dealing with the order in the customer's office. If you don't do this, you may find you need to check something important on the morning of delivery. This can be difficult if you don't have a contact name or number. The form should include all other relevant information such as exactly how to get to a particular place in a large office complex or problems over parking near the place of delivery. If possible encourage customers to place orders by fax or e-mail. It saves staff time – and you have the order in writing in case of any later dispute.

◆ **Have a policy on payment**. One of the joys of a sandwich-coffee bar is that it's a cash business and you don't have to issue invoices. However, outside catering customers will not expect to have to hand over cash for 35 sandwiches. Be organised. Prepare pro-forma invoices on your PC or buy an invoice book from a stationers. Either way make sure you keep copies of what you give to the customer and check them regularly. It's all too easy to forget about outstanding invoices. Make it clear you expect payment within a short time – I suggest a week or two. Contact them if payment is not received. We have found that some larger organisations who give us quite a lot of business have systems whereby invoices are only paid after 30 days. You should probably accept this because you know you will get the money and quite possibly repeat orders.

◆ **Be clear about the extent of the service you are prepared to offer.** Do you want to find yourself providing the sandwiches for a conference on a Saturday afternoon? Or a seminar at 8 o'clock in the evening? Do you want to deliver hot food with its attendant complicating factors? Do you want to consider finger buffets? If so and if you have the freezer space there are a range of products which would fit the bill. Once you are clear in your own mind, be upfront with enquiring customers. Don't be tempted to undertake something problematic on a one-off basis just because it sounds like a nice little earner.

◆ **Do some work on presentation.** Some customers might be perfectly happy with a bagful of sandwiches wrapped in your normal take-away style. However, it really doesn't cost much to impress customers with good presentation. Get hold of some silver platters from the cash and carry. Offer customers the choice of having sandwiches cut in half or quarter – this is easier with some breads than others. This will be appreciated because participants at a seminar for instance will be able to enjoy a selection of your sandwiches. Add a little bit of garnish: sliced tomatoes and seedless grapes with a few leaves of lollo rosso. Put some doyleys underneath the sandwiches and it all looks really professional.

Delivery service for individual customers

The idea here is that customers phone, fax or e-mail orders in by a certain time and you guarantee to deliver sandwiches during a particular time slot. You would, of course, charge for delivery on orders under, say £10, and would restrict delivery to within a certain radius of the shop. I do hear people talking about this kind of service quite a lot but frankly I can see problems.

◆ A lot of people in shops and offices like to get a break at lunchtime and a stroll to their local sandwich-coffee bar fits the bill nicely.
◆ You may well require an extra part-timer or two at lunchtime purely for deliveries.
◆ You will have to spend a fair amount of time on the phone taking orders or checking faxes and e-mails. Given that most people will want their delivery at roughly the same time your delivery driver will have to move fast to fulfil the orders. What's the traffic like in the centre of your town or city at lunchtime?
◆ Will you have to buy one or more vans or motor bikes with the associated insurance and servicing costs? Where will you park them?
◆ Ensuring that you always have the right change for customers could prove a problem.

I'm sure there is a demand for this kind of service, but it's not something you could do half-heartedly. To make a success of it you would need to have high volume and this would mean advertising, investment in suitable equipment and the setting up of an appropriate infrastructure to support the operation.

Perhaps a good compromise would be for customers to place orders in advance which they could then collect at a time of their choosing from an express counter – a bit like getting drinks ordered for the interval at the theatre.

There are now websites you can register with which act as a kind of middle man. Customers place orders with them which are faxed on to you. You then either deliver the order or have it ready to be collected by a particular time.

Much as I respect new technology my instinct is that many people will regard all of this as too much hassle for the simple task of ordering their daily lunch.

Opening more units

If the first one goes well the logic of opening more units can be very seductive. More turnover, more scope for economies of scale – and more money for you. Yes? Well up to a point. *But consider this: if you simply open another shop and try to keep going as before you will simply double your workload.* Will you work part-time in both shops? Will you open and close both shops? What about deliveries between the shops and the extra paperwork? What happens if somebody phones in sick... from two shops? And then there are things like preparing two floats instead of one for the next day. Put like this it doesn't sound very appealing and if you do it this way it won't be.

Opening more units is a big step which needs to be thought through very thoroughly. Firstly, you have to ask yourself some questions.

1. Being honest, do you simply want a small individual business which will provide a reasonable income for a limited number of years, which you can then sell before moving on to something else or perhaps retiring?
2. Do you like the idea of having a good personal relationship with customers?
3. Are you the ambitious, risk-taking, entrepreneurial type?
4. Do you like the idea of finding yourself spending increasing amounts of time looking for alternative sites, negotiating with bankers and talking to solicitors and other advisers?

If your answers are yes to questions 1 and 2 and no to 3 and 4, then opening more units is almost certainly not advisable.

> **If you want to expand, the key skill which you have to develop is delegation. You will not be able to keep direct hands-on control over the day to day running of the shops – especially if you go beyond two units. One of your most important tasks will be to ensure that you choose and promote people who understand your vision – and then make sure they deliver it.**

Having said all this, if you simply want to have *one other outlet* not far from the original one this can probably be achieved by having one reliable manager working full time in the new shop (assuming you want to be heavily involved in the other one). Between you it should be possible to develop systems to make sure that both shops are run efficiently without you taking all the strain.

This idea could be particularly appealing if you came across a small low-cost unit in a good location. It might be feasible to create an 'express' outlet which you stock with ready-made sandwiches from your main shop. You could target particular markets such as morning, mid-morning and lunchtime. It would be necessary to have a good quality coffee machine but nothing other than coffee and tea would need to be made up on the site. An operation like this would need fewer staff and could open for a shorter time each day.

Whatever you decide, if you do expand, there will undoubtedly be more to collect from the cash and carry, more book-keeping to do and perhaps more cooking or baking to be done at home. Accordingly, you may find that you will need someone at assistant manager level to help out in the original shop. You will inevitably have increased staff costs.

Finding a good manager

No matter what, you will undoubtedly have to delegate to some extent, so it's important that you have confidence in the people you choose as managers. Without doubt the best way to get hold of people who can manage the shops is *internal promotion*. In a small business like a sandwich-coffee bar you will know very quickly if a new employee is going to work out as a general assistant. But once they have been working for you for four or five months you will know if they will make good managerial material. Apart from being intimately acquainted with their abilities you will also start to get an idea of their medium to long-term plans. There is no point in setting all of this up if somebody is only planning to stay for a few months.

If someone is happy working for you as an assistant they might well be a lot happier taking on some extra responsibilities in exchange for a pay rise. This need not be massive. It would, of course, be subject to negotiation but an increase of 25 to 30% in their hourly rate may well suffice initially at least.

You could, of course, advertise for a manager in the press. But the applicants would be unknown quantities. You might be lucky. Equally you might find yourself paying a fair bit of money to someone who doesn't see things your way and who might rub your existing staff up the wrong way.

> Assuming you manage to put in place the right staff and create the necessary infrastructure you should be able to have the best of both worlds: achieve a limited expansion of the operation but maintain direct control over the quality of the goods and personal service to your customers.

Ideas for expansion

Another possibility is to consider expansion by opening up in an unusual or apparently undesirable place that other entrepreneurs have overlooked.

> One man has recently opened a café-bar in a railway station in a market town in the south of England. Previous operators had apparently given up because of logistical problems and vandalism. He realised there was a substantial market waiting to be exploited. Having addressed the problems he is trading profitably and is now looking to open more outlets in similarly underexploited spots away from the big centres. What's more, at the weekend he changes the nature of the place with candles and trendy music thus appealing to another more localised market.
>
> Clearly such a course of action has more risks associated with it than opening in a conventional high street location. However, as the market place becomes more crowded it may be increasingly necessary to consider such options. And, of course, fortune favours the brave.

In addition, or alternatively, consider these more modest possibilities:

◆ **Setting up a mobile sandwich and coffee unit** on the pavement in a busy part of town. If you think this sounds a bit far-fetched just take a trip to Manhattan where street vendors are an established part of the scene. And as you know, where America leads, Britain follows. One man in Edinburgh has started to do this (he has even set up miniature coffee and cake outlets in a number of former police boxes would you believe).

Needless to say you will need planning permission for any such venture. You will also have to consider the logistics of having suitable supplies of water and electricity not to mention a nearby toilet for the person who works there.

◆ **Setting up mobile units at major events.** These could range from outdoor music festivals to agricultural shows to fairs. I'm sure I don't need to tell you how poor the standard of catering at such gatherings can be. Yet there is a reasonably affluent captive audience most of whom now expect much higher standards than in the past. Take advantage.

◆ **Come to an arrangement with a larger commercial operation.** There is one chain of coffee shops which has sited units in the high street offices of one of the large banks. Perhaps a gallery, a museum, a department store or your local courts complex would like to offer this sort of facility to its customers but lacks the necessary expertise. If you live in a university town what about somewhere at the heart of the campus? Catch the students as they step blinking into the daylight for breakfast at about 1pm.

◆ **Opening an outlet abroad.** Have you ever come back from a place like Mallorca or Tenerife and thought, 'If only...' Well why not? I've travelled a fair bit and I can tell you that with the possible exception of Manhattan, I have never come across sandwiches anywhere near as good as those available in good sandwich bars in Britain. Indeed a supermarket in the gastronomic capital of the world, Paris, recently advertised the joys of its 'Sandwiches Anglais' which they proudly boasted were made in London and available in Paris three hours later.

If you know how to run a quality sandwich-coffee bar then I think you could well possess a commercial skill for which there would be considerable demand in some of those nice overseas places associated with the tourist trade.

The logistics of acquiring premises and engaging suppliers would no doubt present a few challenges and the trade would to some extent be seasonal. However, if you have the tenacity to do it in Britain I'm sure you can do it abroad as well. An appropriately experienced legal adviser would be crucial.

Empire building

If, having made a clear success of your first two or three units, you want to **start a chain of sandwich-coffee bars** you are into a whole new ball game. Whilst such a venture is beyond the scope of this book there are a number of points to bear in mind:

◆ You can forget all about personal control of what is delivered day to day to the customer. The demands of systems management will make it necessary to reduce sandwiches, tortilla wraps, cakes, etc. to a finite list of customer friendly choices, all carefully sourced, costed, packaged, labelled and portion-controlled. The demands of efficient commerce will almost certainly mean that sandwiches will not be individually made up to order.

◆ Similarly, you can forget the idea of personal contact with the customers. Staff will need to be trained to carry out a range of tasks with maximum efficiency and deliver the corporate vision. Managers will be on a mission to ensure that they do.

◆ Virtually everything you do will require the services of experts. Accountants will be needed to put together a sufficiently detailed business plan; a market research company and/or specialist commercial estate agents will be needed to advise on the suitability of particular sites and locations; consultants in the fields of interior design, refrigeration, food labelling and packaging, lighting, shopfitting, health and hygiene, etc. will be needed.

◆ Apart from independent experts, you will have to put together a management team to deal with the numerous issues which need to be addressed in setting up a substantial commercial operation.

◆ The costs involved will be very considerable indeed – hundreds of thousands if not millions of pounds. It follows that you will need considerable financial backing. Your own bank may well be happy to help but they will refer you to a department dealing specifically with venture capital. Needless to say this is a million miles away from setting up one small independent unit.

Using a Business Angel

Another source of finance for an established small business wanting to expand could be an informal private investor, otherwise known as a 'business angel'. Such people come from all areas of business life. They are usually looking to make a well above average return on a substantial (probably £500,000+) investment, though not necessarily in the short term. They may want to become actively involved in a business as part of their financial investment. Your accountant or business banker might be able to provide help in putting you in touch with one. The British Venture Capital Association, www.bvca.co.uk, tel: 020 7420 1800, publishes a free directory *Sources of Business Angel Capital*. This can be downloaded from their website.

If this sounds exciting and exhilarating, fine. Quite a few people have made fortunes from setting up such operations. Some have expanded overseas and gone into the business of supplying sandwich meals to trains and boats and planes as well as schools.

However, there is not much point in taking on the world until you have learned the ins and outs of the business at entry level.

Becoming a franchisor

There are approximately 30,000 outlets of all kinds run on a franchise basis. It is not an easy option. There is a great deal more to it than just allowing someone to use your name in return for some money.

To begin with you must have a successfully established business with a readily identifiable image, a quality product and a readily repeatable operating system. Each new operation must be such as to allow the franchisee to make a reasonable profit on their investment and pay you a franchise fee which delivers a reasonable return to you. Bear in mind that you will have to:

◆ Provide aftercare, management training and support.

◆ Engage specialist solicitors to draw up franchise documentation.

◆ Put in place arrangements for the bulk purchasing of supplies.

◆ Register your trade marks and trade names.

◆ Ensure that your vision is being delivered and that your franchisees are not cutting corners.

There's no doubt it can be done. Walk into any of the big hamburger chains around the world and it will be virtually identical to the one in your local high street. And it's not just multinational giants. Franchise arrangements have been set successfully by much smaller operations.

Finding out if it's feasible for you will require extensive analysis and development work. You will probably have to engage the services of a franchise consultant. If you are interested you should contact The British Franchise Association on 01235 820470 or obtain further information from their website www.thebfa.org

Selling non-food items

I have already mentioned the possibility of selling paintings by local artists and old photographs of your area. You could also think about souvenirs in tourist areas or perhaps eye-catching pieces of glasswork or T-shirts. For items such as these the only real problem is finding the space and making sure your display is kept smart. You may be able to come to an arrangement with a supplier whereby part of their service is setting up and checking the display on a regular basis and ensuring it looks good.

Don't forget, your principal business is selling sandwiches, so just stock a few items which are attractive and non-perishable.

Supplying other sandwich bars

Like outside catering this appeals because essentially it's a case of more of the same. You might find that a nearby internet café or bookshop would like to offer their customers sandwiches with a cup of coffee but don't have the facilities. Having a daily delivery from you might be just the answer.

If you set up a shop kitchen in your house to produce some sandwich ingredients why not give a few samples to other sandwich bars, wholefood shops or delicatessens? It simply means making more of what you're making already. If demand increases you may have to consider taking on a part-timer to help you. The other issue here is delivery; it will be your responsibility to ensure that products are delivered at the correct temperature. Will you have to buy a refrigerated van, or could you simply get a couple of good quality cool bags?

*In either case you will have to **label** sandwiches or sandwich ingredients in accordance with the relevant regulations – see Chapter Nine.*

Busking

In the world of sandwiches this means going out and about in a car or van with a selection of sandwiches in the back. You go to various places – offices, factories, schools – taking the food to the people rather than the other way around. Since you are permitted to keep sandwiches at ambient temperatures for up to four hours you could do this over the lunchtime period without needing to use a refrigerated vehicle, though a refrigerated vehicle would be far more satisfactory. The idea is to build up a run of places which you service on a daily basis. Particularly if you do have a refrigerated vehicle any sandwiches remaining unsold at, say, 1.30 pm could be returned to the dairy unit in the shop.

Picnic/packed lunch service

This is most likely to be feasible if your shop is in a tourist town or city. Do a mailshot to local hotels, guest houses and bed and breakfasts and try to follow up with phone calls. Visitors phone in orders reasonably early in the morning or the day before and then collect a neatly prepared carrier bag with lots of goodies to last them through the day.

As office people seem to work harder and harder and are less able to leave their desks at set times, there could perhaps be a demand for a similar service whereby somebody could pick up a lunchbox on their way to work. This could be ordered the day before by phone, fax or e-mail.

Developing a delicatessen

You're half-way there already. Your deli unit contains a selection of meats, cheeses, pickles, mayonnaises and so on – and you will, of course, continue to sell ready-made or made-to-order sandwiches as well as coffee and tea. You will, however, have to create refrigerated display space for a wider range of goods. You will also need a lot more places to display an interesting selection of foods and food accompaniments from around the world. This might mean a lot of shelving in imaginative places or some appropriately sized aisle units placed in such a way as to encourage impulse buys. Clearly space will be an issue, though with a bit of imagination you will be surprised at what can be fitted in.

Make it all look busy, extensively stocked and clean. Have things hanging from the ceiling and do what you can to generate some pleasing aromas. Don't allow dust to gather on bottles of raspberry flavoured vinegar which might happen to be slow sellers.

Take a tip: don't just be another small grocer's shop. There are lots of those around already. Make the effort to come up with glamourous looking variations on the theme of good quality food products.

Attending exhibitions, conferences and trade fairs

As the sandwich and coffee industries grow ever larger and more diverse, so do the number of exhibitions, trade fairs and conferences in Britain as well as other European countries.

The British Sandwich Association has its big annual bash in London each year in May. In 2001 there were over 600 guests from all sectors of the industry to cheer as Tim Brooke-Taylor handed out awards for Sandwich Bar of the Year: Independent, New Product of the Year Award, New Sandwich Ingredient of the Year and so on. The BSA also organises the British Sandwich Week with the support of some of the major suppliers. It is accompanied by substantial nationwide advertising and is all aimed at helping to raise the profile of the industry.

To address concerns about southern bias 2001 saw the first Northern Sandwich Show held in the G-Mex Centre in Manchester. There is also an event called the Total Sandwich Show, organised by the British Sandwich Association and held in London in May, which has numerous stands featuring new products and equipment as well as demonstrations of how to make particular sandwiches using innovative techniques.

The BSA also organises conferences which consider the serious issues facing the industry. In 2001 there was a two-day conference in September which included topics such as 'Are Sandwiches Meeting the Needs of Today's Consumers?' and 'Sandwich Bar Retailing – The Importance of Image'.

There are also many competitions which are usually organised by suppliers or manufacturers. One of them, the 'Delifrance European Sandwich Challenge' had in 1999 a first prize of a holiday for two in the south of France. In addition, winners then qualified for a grand final in Paris. For your information, the winner in 1999 was a chef who gave the world this sandwich: barbecued lamb kebab with strawberries and lollo rosso lettuce in a grilled onion baguette. We really have come a long way from bog standard cheese and ham sandwiches.

There is much to learn from all such events. You get the chance to hear new ideas and see new products in action. It all helps to maintain your enthusiasm and keep your own operation buzzing with new ideas. If you go abroad you can combine business with pleasure and the costs will, to some extent at least, be tax-deductible.

Creating your own website

Why not? Lots of people do nowadays. Apart from generating interest in your establishment you will be able to use it as a vehicle for people to place orders. If you are well versed in the world of computers you can do it yourself. In addition there are many companies (see the *Yellow Pages*) which will be happy to set up a site for you. Their charges will range from a few hundred to several thousand pounds and beyond. It's really a question of what size of website and what level of quality you require. Either way you will need an individual domain name. Again, you can do this yourself or pay a specialist company to do it for you.

There are setting up costs and annual charges for a website (which vary according to how much cyberspace you need) and also for the use of your domain name. So the question you have to ask yourself is: Will it be commercially advantageous for me? If you plan to set up a high tech operation with internet-connected computer terminals then it's probably essential.

However, for the average small independent operation starting up it is probably not a justifiable expense. The market you need to attract is the one in the immediate vicinity of your shop, not some insomniac web surfer in Hong Kong.

Another point is that ordering over the internet can actually take a fair amount of time. Having logged on, a customer will have to set up credit card authorisation and give details of a user name and password for future transactions. Businesses which do offer this service will probably have a minimum charge of £20 so that customers will have to band together.

Offering internet access

Without necessarily opening a full-blown internet café it is quite feasible to install a couple of computer terminals which are hooked up to the internet. A good facility to offer in this ever more communication-oriented society. Clearly this will be easier if you are computer literate. Even if you are not there are numerous consultants who can advise you.

There are moves in the catering industry to create units which attract people by being more and more like a comfortable living room or study – and the presence of a computer would undoubtedly help to reinforce this kind of appeal.

You must have at least one member of staff on duty at all times who is reasonably computer/internet literate and able to deal with any problems that arise. It is no good offering a service which you cannot deliver properly. Just think of the frustration caused when a photograph booth doesn't work and the man in the supermarket says it's nothing to do with him.

The other issue is, of course, that time on the computer should be limited and there should be a clear tariff for its use. Otherwise you will get some student hogging the thing for ages and only buying one cup of tea.

I think the future of internet operations in cafés is uncertain for two main reasons which may act to diminish their drawing power:

◆ So many people are online at home now.
◆ Mobile phones will soon be routinely connected to the net.

Despite this, having one or two online computer terminals is always going to be a valuable facility to offer customers.

Selling alcohol

A lot of overseas visitors find it strange that they often cannot buy a beer or a bottle of wine to have with their sandwiches. As moves towards continental eating and drinking customs continue unabated I am sure that pressure for change will increase. It seems an entirely sensible and desirable notion that people should have the option of buying beer and wine. However, as always, the situation is not black and white. Consider these points:

◆ Will there be sufficient demand? Many people who buy sandwiches at lunchtime will be working in the afternoon and will probably not want to drink alcohol.
◆ You will need extra storage space. Not only that but your stocks might now become of interest to the criminal fraternity.
◆ Staff who sell alcohol must be over 18 years of age.
◆ Last but by no means least you will have to apply for a licence to sell alcohol (assuming you do not take over a going concern which already has a licence, in which case you will have to apply to have the existing licence transferred to you).

You will probably need professional assistance from a solicitor experienced in licensing to advise you and help with the paperwork. And obtaining a licence for the first time is by no means a foregone conclusion even if you plan to sell only beer and wine. An initial application will be considered by various interested public bodies including the police and the environmental health and planning departments who will need to be persuaded that yet another outlet selling alcohol is a desirable thing. Procedures vary from place to place but in the first instance you should contact your local council.

And finally

How long should you keep working for? If you set up a chain and become a suit-wearing executive there is really no reason not to keep going until you want or can afford to retire. However, if you choose to be a hands-on proprietor you really should give thought to planning your exit strategy in good time. For example, if you start up your business in your mid thirties then I would say, as a rough guide, you should be thinking about it once you've been going for ten years or so. I say this not because it's a bad way to make a living but rather because of the physical demands it places on you.

It may be that as the years go by and your loans are paid off, you can take on a manager and/or sufficient staff to allow you to take a back seat. This will serve to put back your exit date. However, if you continue to work hands-on you will start to become aware of the fact that you aren't getting any younger. Being on your feet all day, moving trays of juice cans around, going to the cash and carry all take their toll. If at all possible you should aim to get out before your overall health and fitness suffers as a result. I don't want to be overly dramatic about this but I have seen people who have gone on too long and I just don't think it's worth it.

> **Let's face it, you want to enjoy your retirement.**

Oh, one other thing. I haven't given you any ideas for particular sandwiches. Quite right. That's your department. However, I'd like to share with you my own all-time favourite sandwich:

On the outside: walnut bread spread evenly with unsalted butter.

On the inside: pan-fried salmon mixed with mayonnaise, black pepper, a little salt and finely chopped capers; with thick slices of blood red vine tomato, coriander and a mix of cucumber, iceberg and lollo rosso.

Appendices

Extract from Millers staff handbook

DRESS CODE AND PERSONAL HYGIENE

At the present time there is no specific uniform. You should dress simply and smartly. The obvious general rule is don't wear anything which would interfere with your work – e.g. a top with baggy sleeves which might trail in the butter. You will be provided with an apron. Hair should be tied or pinned back. Don't wear perfume or after-shave with a strong scent. Always observe good standards of personal hygiene. No nail-varnish. Discreet jewellery – no rings or bracelets.

USE OF TELEPHONE

The telephone should only be used for business calls. When answering the telephone you should simply say 'Hello, Millers, Hope Park Terrace.'

Personal calls (in or out) should only be made with the permission of Judy or Stephen or in situations of urgency.

ADVERTISING

Throughout the year (but especially during the Edinburgh Festival) people come into the shop wanting to put up posters. In principle there is no objection to this. However the only areas where this is acceptable are as follows:

The area of wall (floor to ceiling) to the left of the front door as you enter. If anyone tries to put posters up elsewhere they should be told not to. The great majority of people are considerate and ask permission to put up posters and offer some free tickets to shows (feel free to ask even if they don't offer). You will however get some people who come into the shop when it's busy and put up posters without asking. Almost invariably they will be the people whose posters we do not want to display and which should be refused – i.e. political posters of one sort or another. In addition, as a general rule we do not accept posters or notices simply advertising commercial products. If in any doubt at all, speak to Judy or Stephen.

NOTE: Posters should only be put up with Blu-tac, NOT Sellotape, drawing pins etc.

USE OF TOILETS BY CUSTOMERS

Since customers are allowed to sit in it follows that they are allowed to use our toilet if they wish. Accordingly the office area should be kept reasonably tidy and access to the toilet should not be impeded. Valuables should not be left lying around.

CHEQUES

A charge of 25p must be added to cheque payments under £10.

Check carefully the following points:

1 Correct date.
2 Correct amount (words and figures).
3 Cheque signed.
4 Check signature against signature on bankers card.
5.Check card expiry date.
6. Write cheque card number AND expiry date on back of cheque (note it is the cheque card number which should be noted on back of cheque, not the account number or sort code number).

CUSTOMERS

Always be consistently pleasant to customers. Nobody feels friendly and outgoing all of the time – we all have personal problems on occasion – however such problems should not be brought into the shop. There are times in the past when difficulties have been created for customers and other members of staff because a particular employee has become withdrawn or sullen for no apparent reason. Such behaviour is not conducive to the smooth running of the shop and is not acceptable.

The general rule is that the customer is always right. However, as with every rule, there will be exceptions and you are not expected to put up with rude or abusive behaviour.

If a customer has a genuine grievance – e.g. finding a hair in a sandwich or buying a carton of milk which is past its sell-by date, the procedure is as follows:

1. Listen to what the customer has to say and show concern.
2. Do not get into a debate or, worse still, an argument.
3. If it is clear that the situation can be easily and reasonably resolved by refunding the price of an unsatisfactory item or providing an alternative item, then do this.
4. However, if it is clear that the situation cannot be resolved in this way, tell the customer that the matter will be dealt with by Judy or Stephen. Ask the customer for a note of his or her name and telephone number and make it clear that somebody will make contact as soon as possible.
5. The aim is to have the matter dealt with as smoothly and quickly as possible in such a way a) that the customer feels that his or her concerns are being properly addressed and, b) that any inconvenience or disturbance to other customers is kept to a minimum.

6. All incidents, major or minor, should be reported to Judy or Stephen at the earliest opportunity – it is a legal requirement that any such incidents are noted.

FRIENDS AND RELATIVES

Whilst your friends are welcome as customers, you should discourage them from socialising with you in the shop, as this creates a bad impression and has the effect of reducing the quality of service to other customers.

POINTS RE MAKING SANDWICHES, PARTICULAR SANDWICH INGREDIENTS, SOUP, MILK ETC.

BASICS

If you are making up a sandwich to order as opposed to for the shelf, ALWAYS offer the customer the following choices:

a. Type of bread or roll.
b. Butter or margarine. (Spread evenly over the whole of both surfaces of the bread or roll – not too thick, not too thin).
c. Type of mayonnaise. (if any).
d. Salt and/or pepper.

Don't express surprise at a particular choice that might seem unusual to you. So far as sandwich ingredients are concerned, the general rule is that you should be fair to the customer and fair to the business – be reasonably generous with ingredients, but not overly so – it's a question of balance. When making up a sandwich to order, the quantity of the main ingredient, meat, cheese or whatever, should be the same as for sandwiches made up for the shelf.

◆ Avoid handling food as much as possible by using tongs etc.
◆ Always use clean knives, clean chopping boards etc to avoid cross-flavouring/ contamination.
◆ Always present a sandwich in an appetising way in the packaging – with the ingredients showing.
◆ If, especially towards the end of the day, you've run out of the thing the customer wants, suggest similar alternatives and make them sound as attractive as possible.

◆ Handle the sandwich as if making it for yourself – i.e. with love and affection and culinary anticipation.

SPECIFIC FOODSTUFFS

◆ AVOCADOS: At any given time there should be a number of avocados in the shop. Before you select one check all of them for ripeness and use the one which is clearly ripest to the touch.

◆ BACON: Cut off any undercooked, non-crispy bits of fat before chopping the bacon.

◆ APPLES, ORANGES, BANANAS AND GRAPEFRUIT: Always rotate the fruit so that the oldest are at the top of the pile. Oranges and grapefruit, which are looking a bit tired and are not of good enough quality to sell individually, can be stored in the fridge and used for juicing. Older bananas can be used for making banana cake.

◆ MUSTARD/HORSERADISH: When making sandwiches up for the shelf which include hot/spicy accompaniments such as mustard or horseradish you have to aim for an average sort of taste – not too much, not too little. If a customer is having a sandwich made up to order, then if he wants enough mustard to set his mouth on fire, that is his privilege.

◆ EGGS: ALWAYS ensure that there is absolutely NO EGGSHELL AND NO SKIN (which are potential sources of salmonella) adhering to the eggs before preparing the egg mayonnaise.

◆ TOMATOES: The tops of tomatoes should be cut off in such a way as to remove most of the husk. The cut-off bits should be retained as they are suitable for making soup.

◆ PRAWNS: Prawns must be defrosted thoroughly and their water discarded. They must be refrigerated as soon as they are defrosted and only removed from the fridge briefly for sandwich preparation. When the serve-over fridge is being cleaned after lunch time any remaining prawns should be placed in the upright fridge, not left out on the side. Prawns should last two days – however if in any doubt, discard them.

◆ SOUP: Soup should be stirred regularly to ensure thorough re-heating and also to avoid it sticking and burning on the bottom of the pan.

◆ COLD MEATS: Trim most of the fat and gristle from ham.

In the case of roast beef watch out for little bits of string the butcher might have failed to remove after cooking.

Smoked turkey sometimes comes with an outer ring of fat and this should be cut off. In general it is helpful to you if the meats are prepared in advance as a batch so that you are not having to, e.g., trim fat off individual slices of ham at a time when the shop is busy and you are under pressure.

Chicken breasts are delivered whole and require to be sliced. Try to do this as consistently as possible. The slices should be of reasonable thickness but not overly generous. The accompanying sauces should be retained and poured over the sliced chicken breasts.

As with all fresh ingredients the rule about rotation is very important.

When cold meats are received from the butcher they must be dated and labelled. When meats are two/three days old they must be discarded. If in any doubt speak to Judy.

◆ MILK AND YOGHURT: Milk is delivered two or three times a week usually just as the shop is opening. The delivery man takes the milk out of the crate and places the cartons on the floor. In order to ensure that the milk stays fresh for as long as possible it is important that the milk is put in the fridge without delay. The rule about rotation is particularly important. The cartons should be placed in the fridge with their sell-by dates clearly visible to customers (apart from being good practice, this discourages the customers from handling the cartons whilst attempting to check the sell-by date).

In general, the foregoing points apply to yoghurts.

The sell-by dates of all milk and yoghurt products should be checked on a daily basis.

◆ OUTSIDE CATERING: At the present time we do not do a great deal of outside catering but it is an area we are keen to develop. Accordingly any inquiries from customers should be met with enthusiasm.

Useful contacts and publications

Business Start-Ups - Advice Lines

England – Business Link: 0845 6009006

Wales – Business Link: 029 2036 8483

Scotland – Small Business Gateway: 0845 6096611

Northern Ireland – Business Link: 02890 239090

(Also contact local councils and colleges for details of current initiatives and courses)

The British Franchise Association

Thames View, Newtown Road, Henley-on-Thames, Oxon RG9 1HG

Tel: 01865 379892 • Fax: 01491 573517 • www.thebfa.org

The British Sandwich Association

Association House, 18c Moor Street, Chepstow NP16 5DB

Tel: 01291 636333 • www.sandwich.org.uk

Employment Law and Related Matters

The government has helpfully gathered a large amount of information in the following website: www.direct.gov.uk Log on to the site and enter your chosen topic in the search box to obtain up to date relevant information.

New Employer's Helpline

Tel: 0845 915 4515.

Federation of Small Businesses

Sir Frank Whittle Way, Blackpool Business Park, Blackpool, FY4 2FE

Tel: 01253 348046 • www.fsb.org.uk

ACAS (Advisory Conciliation & Arbitration Service)

See local telephone directory for nearest office.

Food Hygiene

A large amount of information including links to other sites is available at the website of the Food Standards Agency: www.food.gov.uk

Courses on food hygiene are run by various organisations including:

◆ Chartered Institute of Environmental Health
◆ The Royal Institute of Public Health and Hygiene
◆ The Royal Society of Health
◆ The Royal Environmental Health Institute of Scotland
◆ Society of Food Hygiene Technology.

In addition, your local Environmental Health Officer will have information on courses in your area.

Health and Safety

Visit the website for the Health and safety Executive which contains relevant information and links: www.hse.gov.uk

All Tax Matters

Visit the website of HM Revenue and customs: www.hmrc.gov.uk or contact your local tax office.

Institute of Chartered Accountants

(For details of local accountants specialising in small businesses)
See local telephone directory for nearest office.

Law Society

(For details of local solicitors specialising in small businesses)
See local telephone directory for nearest office.

Luncheon Vouchers

New sales enquiries – tel: 0845 3651217

Organic Food

For enquiries relating to organic food visit the website of the Department for Environment Food and Rural Affairs (DEFRA) www.defra.gov.uk

Performing Rights Society

Copyright House, 29-33 Berners St, London W1T 3AB

020 7580 5544 • Fax: 020 7306 4455 • www.prsformusic.com

Phonographic Performance Ltd

1 Upper James Street, London WIF 9DE

Tel: 020 7534 1000 • www.ppluk.com

Royal National Institute For The Blind (Ask for transcription service)

See local telephone directory for nearest office.

International Sandwich and Snack News The British Sandwich Association

Association House, 18c Moor Street, Chepstow NP16 5DB

Tel: 01291 636333 • www.sandwich.org.uk

Venture Capital
British Venture Capital Association

Tel: 020 7420 1800 • www.bvca.co.uk

Further reading

There is not a large body of literature specifically relevant to sandwich-coffee bars. One of the best sources of information about new trends or developments is undoubtedly the trade magazine, *International Sandwich and Snack News* and its sister magazine *Café*. The cost of subscription is modest (and tax deductible). You can also buy back issues on subjects of particular interest to you.

Similarly, if you become a member of the Federation of Small Businesses, they publish two magazines, *First Voice* and *Business Network* which contain information of wider interest to people running their own businesses. Full details can be found in Useful Contacts and Publications.

Apart from these magazines there are a number of books on particular aspects of setting up and running businesses. How To Books publish a number of relevant titles:

◆ *Preparing a Winning Business Plan*
◆ *Starting Your Own Business*
◆ *Book-keeping and Accounting For The Small Business*
◆ *The Small Business Start-up Workbook.*

In addition don't underestimate the importance of reading cookery books and magazines. You're in a competitive field and it's important to spot new trendy tastes, and to find ways of introducing them into your repertoire. It's all part of the important business of staying ahead of the game.

Index

SOME OTHER TITLES FROM HOW TO BOOKS

85 INSPIRING WAYS TO MARKET YOUR SMALL BUSINESS
Inspiring, self-help, sales and marketing strategies that you can apply to your own business immediately

JACKIE JARVIS

This book is for the many people who run their own small to medium-sized business and who want to make it grow. It sets out to be your own, pocket, marketing consultant – without the expense. Not only does it offer some great ideas but it explains how each idea will benefit your business, what you need to do to make it work, and how you can apply it to your own business immediately.

ISBN 978-1-84528-396-4

THE SMALL BUSINESS START-UP WORKBOOK

CHERYL D. RICKMAN

'I would urge every business adviser in the land to read this book' – Sylvia Tidy-Harris, Managing Director of www.womenspeakers.co.uk

'Inspirational and practical workbook that takes you from having a business idea to actually having a business. By the time you have worked through the exercises and checklists you will be focussed, confident and raring to go.' – www.allthatwomenwant.co.uk

'A real 'must have' for anyone thinking of setting up their own venture.' – Thames Valley News

'... a very comprehensive book, a very readable book.' – Sister Business E-Zine

ISBN 978-1-84528-038-3

WAKE UP AND SMELL THE PROFIT

52 guaranteed ways to make more money in your coffee business

JOHN RICHARDSON WITH HUGH GILMARTIN

Witty, authoritative, comprehensive and fun, *Wake Up and Smell the Profit* is the ultimate guide to making more money in your coffee business.

With 52 motivating tips and suggestions (plus an extra bonus idea for good measure), all you need to do is apply one initiative a week for a year and you could have a much more profitable and easier to manage business within twelve months.

With this book you'll be able to:

- Make more money and work less
- Have happier customers who spend more money
- Win more customers without spending a fortune
- Enjoy running your business more
- Create customers who rave about your business and consequently generate more customers through word of mouth

ISBN 978-1-84528-334-6

MASTERING BOOK-KEEPING

DR PETER MARSHALL

An accredited textbook of The Institute of Chartered Bookkeepers.

This updated 8th edition contains extracts from ICB, AAT, OCR and AQA sample examination papers.

'This book has been planned to cover the requirements of all the major examining boards' syllabuses and achieves all it sets out to do.' Focus on Business Education

'Presented in a clear and logical manner – written in plain English.'
Learning Resources News

'This book has great potential value.' Educational Equipment Magazine

ISBN 978-1-84528-324-7

ORDERING

How To Books are available through all good bookshops, or you can order direct from us through Grantham Book Services.

Tel: +44 (0)1476 541080
Fax: +44 (0)1476 541061
Email: orders@gbs.tbs-ltd.co.uk

Or via our website
www.howtobooks.co.uk

To order via any of these methods please quote the title(s) of the book(s) and your credit card number together with its expiry date.

For further information about our books and catalogue, please contact:
How To Books
Spring Hill House
Spring Hill Road
Begbroke
Oxford
OX5 1RX

Visit our web site at
www.howtobooks.co.uk

Or you can contact us by email at info@howtobooks.co.uk